Habits *of* Mind
Across the Curriculum

ASCD cares about Planet Earth.
This book has been printed
on environmentally friendly paper.

Habits *of* Mind

Across the Curriculum

Practical and Creative Strategies for Teachers

Edited by

Arthur L. Costa and Bena Kallick

Association for Supervision and Curriculum Development • Alexandria, Virginia USA

Association for Supervision and Curriculum Development
1703 N. Beauregard St. • Alexandria, VA 22311-1714 USA
Phone: 800-933-2723 or 703-578-9600 • Fax: 703-575-5400
Web site: www.ascd.org • E-mail: member@ascd.org
Author guidelines: www.ascd.org/write

Gene R. Carter, *Executive Director*; Nancy Modrak, *Publisher*; Julie Houtz, *Director of Book Editing & Production*; Darcie Russell, *Project Manager*; Georgia Park, *Senior Graphic Designer*; Mike Kalyan, *Production Manager*; Barton Matheson Willse & Worthington, *Typesetter*; Sarah Plumb, *Production Specialist*

All Web links in this book are correct as of the publication date below but may have become inactive or otherwise modified since that time. If you notice a deactivated or changed link, please e-mail books@ascd.org with the words "Link Update" in the subject line. In your message, please specify the Web link, the book title, and the page number on which the link appears.

PAPERBACK ISBN: 978-1-4166-0763-2   ASCD product #108014   n1/09
Also available as an e-book through ebrary, netLibrary, and many online booksellers (see Books in Print for the ISBNs).

Quantity discounts for the paperback edition only: 10–49 copies, 10%; 50+ copies, 15%; for 1,000 or more copies, call 800-933-2723, ext. 5634, or 703-575-5634. For desk copies: member@ascd.org.

Library of Congress Cataloging-in-Publication Data

Habits of mind across the curriculum : practical and creative strategies for teachers / [edited by] Arthur L. Costa, Bena Kallick.
   p. cm.
Includes bibliographical references and index.
ISBN 978-1-4166-0763-2 (pbk. : alk. paper) 1. Thought and thinking—Study and teaching. 2. Curriculum planning. I. Costa, Arthur L. II. Kallick, Bena.

LB1590.3.H33 2009
370.15′2—dc22

2008042598

18 17 16 15 14 13 12 11 10 09   1 2 3 4 5 6 7 8 9 10 11 12

This collection of writings is dedicated to the many teachers, administrators, and parents in the numerous schools and communities throughout the world who have adopted and implemented the Habits of Mind and have found them to be a meaningful way to organize learning. The future world will be a more thoughtful, compassionate, and cooperative place because of their dedication to cultivating the Habits of Mind in students and modeling them in their own behavior.

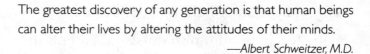

The greatest discovery of any generation is that human beings
can alter their lives by altering the attitudes of their minds.
—*Albert Schweitzer, M.D.*

Habits of Mind Across the Curriculum

Practical and Creative Strategies for Teachers

Preface

> The story—from *Rumpelstiltskin* to *War and Peace*—is one of the
> basic tools invented by the human mind for the purpose of under-
> standing. There have been great societies that did not use the
> wheel, but there have been no societies that did not tell stories.
>
> —*Ursula K. Le Guin*

The network of teachers and schools that are practicing the Habits of
Mind increases daily. We hear from teachers from all over the world,
including teachers in formalized networks in Australia, New Zealand,
Singapore, Sweden, Hong Kong, and England, and in informal networks
in the United States. Our Web site (http://www.habits-of-mind.net/) has
been a place of exchange for many of these educators who share our vision
of a fundamental set of behaviors for thoughtful teaching and learning.

The stories in this book mark a place in the ongoing narrative of
changing classrooms into thoughtful places. As teachers describe their
ways of introducing and sustaining the Habits of Mind, they are providing a vision of what is possible at a time when we too easily forget that the
real purpose of education is to create a critical, discerning, and creative
citizenship for the future of democracy.

FIGURE I

Habits of Mind

Persisting
Stick to it! Persevering in a task through completion; remaining focused; looking for ways to reach your goal when stuck; not giving up.

Managing impulsivity
Take your time! Thinking before acting; remaining calm, thoughtful, and deliberative.

Listening with understanding and empathy
Understand others! Devoting mental energy to another person's thoughts and ideas; making an effort to perceive another's point of view and emotions.

Thinking flexibly
Look at it another way! Being able to change perspectives, generate alternatives, consider options.

Thinking about your thinking (metacognition)
Know your knowing! Being aware of your own thoughts, strategies, feelings, and actions, and their effects on others.

Striving for accuracy
Check it again! Always doing your best; setting high standards; checking and finding ways to improve constantly.

Questioning and posing problems
How do you know? Having a questioning attitude; knowing what data are needed and developing questioning strategies to produce those data; finding problems to solve.

Applying past knowledge to new situations
Use what you learn! Accessing prior knowledge; transferring knowledge beyond the situation in which it was learned.

Thinking and communicating with clarity and precision
Be clear! Striving for accurate communication in both written and oral form; avoiding overgeneralizations, distortions, deletions, and exaggerations.

Gathering data through all senses
Use your natural pathways! Paying attention to the world around you; gathering data through taste, touch, smell, hearing, and sight.

Creating, imagining, and innovating
Try a different way! Generating new and novel ideas, fluency, originality.

Responding with wonderment and awe
Have fun figuring it out! Finding the world awesome and mysterious; being intrigued with phenomena and beauty.

Taking responsible risks
Venture out! Being adventuresome; living on the edge of your competence; trying new things constantly.

Finding humor
Laugh a little! Finding the whimsical, incongruous, and unexpected; being able to laugh at yourself.

Thinking interdependently
Work together! Being able to work with and learn from others in reciprocal situations; working in teams.

Remaining open to continuous learning
I have so much more to learn! Having humility and pride when admitting you don't know; resisting complacency.

This book provides an entry point for seeing through the lens of practice how to introduce and sustain the habits. The stories tell how teachers get started, how they integrate the habits into their curriculum, and how they have changed their ways of planning for curriculum through building lessons and units of study incorporating the habits. We suggest using visualization as one means to familiarize students with the Habits of Mind. To that end, we've included icons related to the Habits of Mind in Figure 1 (see p. x).

Although it might be easy to think of the habits as a set of behaviors that we want students to have so that we can get on with the curriculum that we need to cover, it becomes apparent that we need to provide specific opportunities for students to practice the habits. Habits are formed only through continuous practice. And to practice the habits, our curriculum, instruction, and assessments must provide generative, rich, and provocative opportunities for using them. So, for example, when we are concerned about persistence, we need to provide the kinds of problems and rich tasks that engage students and hold their attention long enough for persistence to be important. When we are concerned with the habit of metacognition, we need to provide opportunities for students to plan for, monitor, thoughtfully reflect upon, and become explicitly aware of how they are thinking. We, as teachers, need to interact with their metacognitive thinking so that we understand better how to reach each student and motivate learning. We need to continuously be asking, what have we done today that creates the opportunity for expressing wonderment and awe? Has there been a problem, an event, an observation that really deserves the exclamation "Awesome!"?

Our Purpose in This Book

The intent of this collection is to provide a wide array of models of lessons. The models are not intended to be adopted or copied per se, but rather to serve as a stimulus for further development of additional lessons in a variety of content areas with diverse populations of students. We encourage schools and school districts to begin to collect archives of such locally developed and tested lessons that may be used for professional study groups, as models to orient new staff members, and to celebrate masterful accomplishments of the craft of teaching.

This book serves as an additional resource for teachers who are learning to implement the Habits of Mind. It builds upon the previous works on the Habits of Mind by Arthur L. Costa and Bena Kallick—namely, *Habits of Mind: A Developmental Series* (2000), which consists of the following volumes: *Discovering and Exploring Habits of Mind, Activating and Engaging Habits of Mind, Assessing and Reporting on Habits of Mind*, and *Integrating and Sustaining Habits of Mind*. And it is meant to accompany the most recent publication: *Learning and Leading with Habits of Mind* (2008), all published by the Association for Supervision and Curriculum Development.

The collection of stories presented in this book demonstrates that teachers deliberately adopt and assess Habits of Mind as outcomes of their curriculum and instruction. Focusing on, teaching, and encouraging growth in the Habits of Mind can change the design of their activities, determine their selection of content, and enlarge their assessments. The collection also illustrates that there are many ways to teach the habits. You are encouraged to refer to Chapter 5 "Is Your Instruction Habit Forming?" in *Learning and Leading with Habits of Mind*, where you will find several approaches to designing lessons with Habits of Mind in mind.

How the Book Is Organized

In this book we have carried over and updated some of the chapters from our earlier book *Activating and Engaging Habits of Mind*. And we have added new chapters, most of which represent a different discipline and developmental age group.

After laying the groundwork in Chapter 1, we move on in Chapter 2 to a delightful piece by Nick D'Aglas of Victoria, Australia, whose culinary skills have obviously improved with the Habits of Mind. His survey may also serve as a review of the 16 habits.

We are often asked, "Where do I start?" In Chapter 3, Lisa Davis-Miraglia suggests you start with your own students and gives many classroom examples of how to begin.

Alan Cooper and Georgette Jenson from New Zealand get down to specifics in Chapter 4 and present helpful ways to make the Habits of

Mind more meaningful to students. Their suggestions apply to students at any grade level or in any area of content.

Many students will be unfamiliar with the Habits of Mind in terms of their meanings and the skills and strategies necessary to apply them. Chapter 5 includes many suggestions for ways to teach the habits. We include this to demonstrate that we not only "infuse" the habits into content instruction; we also must teach these habits explicitly. The chapter explains each of the Habits of Mind and includes strategies for their development. As teachers, you will want to add to these suggestions and bring your own creativity, experiences, and knowledge to bear.

You are then taken on a grand tour of lesson types, visiting the Habits of Mind at several grade levels and seeing how they can be applied in commonly taught school subjects: reading, social studies, the performing arts, math, foreign language, character education, poetry, and physical education.

Because the separation of the disciplines may deter transfer, we include a reminder in Chapter 19 from James Anderson about the need to apply learnings across the disciplines. The separation of the disciplines may produce episodic, compartmentalized, and encapsulated thinking in students. When the biology teacher says, "Today we're going to learn to spell some biology terms," students often respond by saying, "Spelling—in biology? No way!" In this mindset, biology has little meaning for physical education, which has no application to literature and even less connection to algebra. The goal may be incorrectly viewed as the need to master a series of subjects rather than to habituate the search for meaningful relationships and to apply knowledge beyond the context in which it was learned. The Habits of Mind transcend episodic, separated thinking.

As with so many educational initiatives, it may be easy to get started with the Habits of Mind but difficult to sustain the effort. (You've probably heard statements such as this: "Outcomes-based education—we did that last year.") Habits of Mind, however, is not another program to be added to an already overcrowded curriculum. Rather, like a tapestry, it is woven into curriculum, instruction, and assessment. Chapter 20, "Sustaining a Focus on the Habits of Mind," provides many suggestions for sustaining the Habits of Mind over time.

How to Read This Book

The book is not meant to be read in a linear fashion. Rather, each story stands on its own, replete with examples that might inspire your own practice. We suggest that you not limit yourself to reading the story that matches your subject matter. Rather, read the stories for the experience and insight they convey.

All the stories reveal each author's dedication to students' acquisition of these lifelong, enduring, and essential learnings. The goal is to guide students toward success in their future, which in turn will create a more "thought-full," cooperative, and compassionate world.

As you read the stories, consider how you might adopt—or adapt—something that would work well for both you and your students. And finally, create your own story.

❖   ❖   ❖

Acknowledgments

We wish to acknowledge the encouragement and support of the publications staff at ASCD, including Scott Willis, Nancy Modrak, and Darcie Russell; also the excellent work of Kathleen Florio.

We also wish to express our appreciation to all the dedicated professionals who have contributed their knowledge, creativity, and talents to this book. Their main beneficiaries, of course, are their students.

We pay particular tribute to Bena's husband, Charles, and Art's wife, Nancy, who tolerated our time away from them. Their love, encouragement, and understanding provided the support base for our success.

1

Habit Is a Cable

Arthur L. Costa and Bena Kallick

Habit is a cable; we weave a thread of it each day, and at last we cannot break it.

—*Horace Mann*

While visiting a school that had implemented the Habits of Mind for several years, a 4th grade student approached and announced, "I think you need to have another Habit of Mind!"

"Wonderful," was the reply. "And what might that be?"

"Be nice to each other," he wisely suggested and ran off to class.

Although 16 Habits of Mind have been identified and described, that does not mean the list is complete. It is a work in progress that is richly informed by the work of students and teachers in classrooms all over the world.

Since the first volumes describing the Habits of Mind were published, numerous schools in countries around the world have adopted them and infused them into their curriculum, instruction, assessments, and school culture. As many teachers claim, "They just make sense!"

Whenever we ask teachers to describe what they see students doing and hear them saying that indicates the students do not seem to be inclined to think skillfully, they generate a long list of their frustrations.

When we ask them to describe how they would like their students to be, however, they usually generate a list that looks like this:

- Be independent thinkers; think before they act.
- Be more self-motivated.
- Be more inquisitive.
- Pay attention to detail; take pride in work.
- Be more diligent and persistent.
- Enjoy working through the work.
- Think for themselves; not always follow another's lead.
- Generate their own thoughts.
- Be self-directed; use strategies of problem solving.
- Transfer knowledge and apply to new situations.
- Have confidence; be able to take risks.
- Support answers so that they can show evidence of their thinking.
- Communicate with each other; work it out together.

When we introduce teachers to the Habits of Mind and ask them to compare their list of desirable attributes with the attributes described in the Habits of Mind, the insight occurs. It is no wonder that the habits make so much sense. They represent what we have all been looking for in our students, and they provide a common language and vision for what we would like our students to become as they go through our educational process. Furthermore, teachers discover that the habits not only are good for the students but also serve the adults in the school culture. Soon staff members start to ask the critical questions: How can we effectively bring these habits into our school? How can I incorporate the Habits of Mind into my teaching and lesson design?

The Stories Within the Curriculum

Habits of Mind Across the Curriculum: Practical and Creative Strategies for Teachers focuses on the innovative practices that teachers have uncovered as they answer these questions. The lessons learned from these teachers' experiences reveal several stories. One is the story of the transdisciplinary nature of the Habits of Mind. By *transdisciplinary*, we mean that there is no "subject matter" to the Habits of Mind; rather, they are applicable in *every* subject matter. Whether you are teaching reading, science, math, foreign language, or physical education, the Habits of Mind can be applied. To be successful, athletes, for example, must persist, manage their impulsivity, metacogitate, and strive for accuracy. The same is true for musicians, scientists, artists, and mathematicians.

Another story is of shared vision. Schools do not expect that all teachers will teach the same content in the same way or at the same time. A shared vision, however, means that all the staff members share a vision of the desired dispositions of their students, and they use their content as a vehicle to help students achieve those dispositions. To ensure this outcome as students travel from class to class in secondary school or from grade to grade in elementary school, the Habits of Mind must be encountered and reinforced repeatedly. Students will more likely habituate and internalize these dispositions if the benefits are promoted throughout the school, in every subject area, as well as at home and in the community.

Yet another story is of a curriculum map that shows the use of the Habits of Mind in an articulated and coherent way. If these dispositions are valued, then upon completion of their school experiences, students should have encountered and internalized all of them according to an organized plan.

The final story is one of increasing complexity over time. As students progress through the grades, they not only will become aware of the powerful meanings of the Habits of Mind, they also will become more skillful in their use of the habits; they will recognize the habits' merits and values, use them more spontaneously in an increasingly wider set of situations, and become more self-evaluative in their use of the habits. The ultimate but never fully achieved goal is for students to internalize the Habits of Mind, to use them as an internal compass to guide their thoughts, decisions, and actions in their school learning as well as their daily lives. Realizing this, school staffs need to plan lessons accordingly, so that as students mature in their inclination, skill, spontaneous use, and wider application of the Habits of Mind, instruction will mature in a corresponding fashion.

FIGURE 1.1
Four Levels of Educational Outcomes

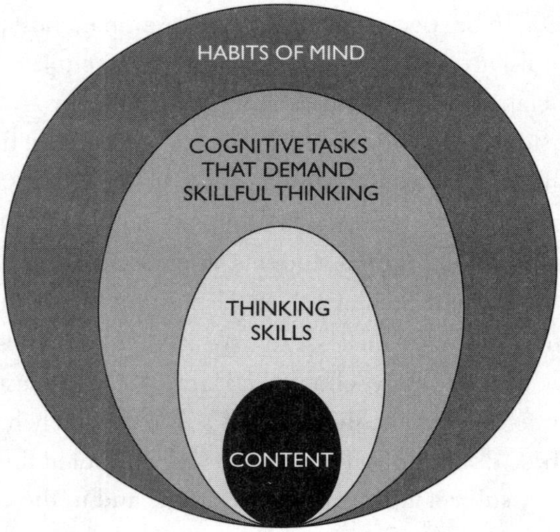

Source: From *Learning and Leading with Habits of Mind* (p. 48), by A. L. Costa & B. Kallick, 2008, Alexandria, VA: Association for Supervision and Curriculum Development. Copyright © 2008 by ASCD. Reprinted with permission.

Habits of Mind in the Curriculum

The Habits of Mind serve as the warp for the curriculum, and the courses of study serve as the weft. *Habits of Mind Across the Curriculum: Practical and Creative Strategies for Teachers* provides many examples of how the tapestry develops in various contexts.

While planning lessons, teachers make decisions about curriculum, instructional methodologies, and assessment strategies, and they hold in their minds at least four nested levels of outcomes. Each one is broader and more encompassing than the level within, and each represents greater authenticity. Figure 1.1 summarizes these outcomes, which we discuss in more detail in the sections that follow. Skillful teachers learn to maintain the vision of the whole as they work in each level simultaneously.

Content

The work of instructional design starts by answering questions such as this: What concepts and principles do we want students to learn? State, provincial, and school district standards of learning often help with this decision. Day-to-day learning activities are now used as vehicles to learn content. Teachers ask questions such as these:

- What concepts or understandings do I want my students to know as a result of this activity?
- What will I do to help them understand?
- How will I know they understand the concepts?

Thinking Skills

Content, however, is not the end of the process. Standards also apply to thinking skills and abilities that students are expected to display. Types of thinking are often embedded in subject matter standards that use specific thinking verbs to describe what students are to do in meeting the content standard (for example, "*analyze* the differences" between two kinds of government, or "*draw conclusions*" from a certain kind of experiment). Thus the content becomes a vehicle for experiencing, practicing, and applying the processes needed to think creatively and critically: observing and collecting data, formulating and testing hypotheses, drawing conclusions, and posing questions.

Such standards suggest that successful instruction in skillful thinking should be done *while* teaching subject matter instead of *in addition to* teaching subject matter. Thinking and subject matter content are neither separate from nor in opposition to each other. The implication is that a student cannot demonstrate mastery of any of these required standards without performing one or more important thinking skills. At this level, teachers address questions such as these:

- What processes do I want my students to practice and develop?
- What thinking skills will be required to activate the mind about the big ideas I am presenting?
- How can I directly teach those thinking skills and processes?

Cognitive Tasks That Demand Skillful Thinking

The Habits of Mind are drawn forth in response to problems, the answers to which are not immediately known. Teachers, therefore, design rich tasks requiring strategic thinking, long-range planning, creating something new, making a decision, resolving discrepancies, clarifying ambiguities, constructing the meaning of a phenomenon, conducting research to test theories, or ameliorating polarities. If the task is not sufficiently authentic, engaging, and challenging, then students will revert to merely reproducing knowledge. When students are sufficiently challenged, they give meaning to the work, produce new knowledge, and draw upon the Habits of Mind.

Habits of Mind

From the broadest perspective, students not only must use the Habits of Mind to succeed in the cognitive task that is assigned; they also must learn that success is ensured by mindfully applying these habits. Teachers might alert students to the need for employing and monitoring certain Habits of Mind as they engage in the task. Through reflection and self-evaluation, they begin to see how the application of the habits transfers to all subject areas. As they work through a cognitively demanding task, they experience the need for interdependent thinking, persisting, drawing upon past knowledge, and other habits. Finally, upon completion of the task, students think about their thinking. They might be asked reflective questions such as these:

• What metacognitive strategies did you employ to manage and monitor your listening skills during your work in teams?

• What effect did striving for accuracy and precision have on your product?

• How did thinking interdependently contribute to your task accomplishment?

Questions might also be asked to invite transfer to situations beyond this learning:

• In what other classes would it be important to strive for accuracy and precision?

• In what other situations beyond school would thinking interdependently contribute to your success?

This attention leads to a process of internalization. Continuous explicit reference to the habits, practice in applying the habits in their work, identifying and analyzing the skills underlying each of the habits, and appreciating the value that the habits bring to their lives lead to students finally making the habits part of all that they do.

The Ultimate Goals

Knowledge, as traditionally taught and tested in school subjects, often consists of a mass of content that is not understood deeply enough to enable a student to think critically in the subject and to seek and find relationships with other subjects. Immersion in a discipline will not necessarily produce learners who have the ability to transfer the concepts and principles of the discipline into everyday life situations. Students acquire the idea that they learn something for the purpose of passing the test rather than accumulating wisdom and personal meaning from the content. It is our desire that the Habits of Mind will serve as a link among the various disciplines so that students will find the connections, bridges, and unifying themes of learning across content areas.

Probably the most influential way in which students learn the Habits of Mind, however, is through their teachers' modeling. Students learn best through imitation of the significant adults around them. Furthermore, the Habits of Mind are as good for the adults in the school as they are for the students. We all can get better at them. We all can apply them in making not only our schools and classrooms but also our homes, communities, and nations more "thought-full" places.

2

Cooking Habits

Nicholas D'Aglas

Editors' note: Successful people in all professions use the Habits of Mind—consciously or unconsciously—during the course of their work. Here, author Nicholas D'Aglas shows how chefs might use the habits when preparing a meal and refining their skills.

Persisting
- Try and try again.
- Continue the task, especially when the outcome is not clear.

Managing Impulsivity

- Take time to read the recipe.
- Prepare equipment and collect ingredients.
- Read the recipe again before beginning.

Listening with Understanding and Empathy

- Ask how your cooking partner feels about the different parts of the task.
- Ask yourself, "Am I in the mood for production?"

Thinking Flexibly

- Ask yourself, "What ingredients could I substitute?"
- Ask yourself, "What equipment could I substitute?"

Thinking About Thinking (Metacognition)

- Reflect on your organizational skills.
- Evaluate your approach to production tasks.

Striving for Accuracy

- Tick off the ingredients as you collect them.
- Tick off the steps in the method.
- Weigh and measure carefully.

Questioning and Posing Problems

- Ask yourself, "What is available and in season?"
- Ask yourself, "Why was the result successful or unsuccessful?"
- Ask yourself, "How could the taste, texture, or appearance of the dish be improved?"

Applying Past Knowledge to New Situations
- Ask yourself, "Have I made something similar?"
- Ask yourself, "Do I have an old recipe for this dish?"

Thinking and Communicating with Clarity and Precision
- Know the names and uses of pieces of equipment.
- Know the names of different methods and production techniques.

Gathering Data Through All Senses
- Taste throughout production and assembly.
- Feel and look for appropriate texture.
- Smell for aroma during and after the process.

Creating, Imagining, Innovating

- Change recipes to suit different clients.
- Garnish and present food in different ways.

Responding with Wonderment and Awe

- Find out about recipes from other countries and cultures.
- Explore new taste sensations.
- Love the production process and the associated skills.

Taking Responsible Risks

- Try different foods.
- Be flexible about cooking times.
- Try unusual flavor combinations.

Finding Humor

- Remember that even the best chefs make mistakes.
- Don't get too upset if things go wrong.

Thinking Interdependently

- Ask others about their experiences.
- Share production roles.

Remaining Open to Continuous Learning

- Learn new things.
- Explore the food industry.
- Investigate different diets.
- Discover different cooking techniques.

3

Start with
Your Own Students

Lisa Davis-Miraglia

Perhaps you feel you're ready to begin using the Habits of Mind with your own students. As you observe them working in groups, solving problems, and interacting with others, which Habits of Mind do you think they need most? You might ask yourself, "What is it about my students that makes me think they need to learn how to think? What do I see them doing, hear them saying, or notice them feeling that indicates they need to learn these Habits of Mind? How would I like them to be?"

I do not suggest you start with all 16 of the habits described in this book. Prioritize the list. Share the list with your class and discuss what certain Habits of Mind would look or sound like if students used them. Are your students impulsive, acting without thinking and blurting out answers? You may wish to start with managing impulsivity. Do your students interrupt each other, laugh at others, or put them down? You may wish to start with the habit of listening with understanding and empathy. Do your students lack awareness of their own problem-solving strategies and their effects on others? You may wish to begin with thinking about thinking (metacognition).

I begin to use the Habits of Mind in conversation with my students when school starts. I begin the year by immersing the children in cooperative activities that require them to problem solve from the moment they walk in the door. For example, the following problem is written on the board on the first day of school: "You may sit at any table provided you meet the following criteria: There is only one person from your class last year, and your table must be mixed by gender." This problem gives all the students something to do when they come in, which relieves some of the first-day jitters.

When the children finish solving a problem, we discuss what happened. One of the most important things for children to do in school is reflect, especially after cooperative tasks and long-term projects. To truly understand a concept, students need time to question, explore, refine their thinking, observe, and reflect. Unfortunately, this "think time" tends to be the first thing to go when time is short.

In the beginning of the year, I start the reflective discussions by telling the children what I observed as I was "kidwatching." (As the year progresses the children lead the discussion.) After the children completed the first-day problem, for example, I noted that Dillon and Matt were very *persistent* because they wanted to sit together, as did Jessa and Lauren. This table of four students met the mixed-gender criterion, but something still wasn't working.

I asked, "Can you tell us what happened?" Dillon explained, "Matt, Lauren, and I were all in the same class last year, but the only other people that we could trade with also had people that had been in the same class."

Matt clarified, "The problem is that 11 out of 23 of us had Mr. Hill last year. So that means every table will have to have two kids from Mr. Hill's class, and one table will have to have three from his class." I asked how they resolved the issue.

Jessa said, "The boys suggested that we do Rock, Paper, Scissors. But then Lauren said she would be willing to sit at this [the neighboring] table as long as I could sit directly across the aisle from her."

Lauren said, "I would have done Rock, Paper, Scissors, but that would have only solved our problem. It wouldn't have solved the whole-class problem of putting two kids from Mr. Hill's class at each table."

I thanked the four of them for sharing what went well and what was difficult for them. I emphasized that thinking about everyone in the community was especially impressive. Then I specifically thanked Jessa and

Lauren for *taking that risk* on the first day of school. I emphasized that I know how important it is to be near someone you're comfortable with.

This short exercise required problem solving and cooperation. It was also an opportunity for me to start identifying behaviors that I would be looking for in the future.

4

Practical Processes
for Teaching Habits of Mind

Alan Cooper and Georgette Jenson

Even if you're on the right track, you'll get run over if you just sit there.

—*Will Rogers*

This chapter presents practical, straightforward processes that have been tested and used in real classroom situations. It describes various actions for implementing the Habits of Mind in the classroom and thereby preparing students for lifelong learning. The actions should not, however, be seen as either prescriptive or definitive. They are starting points. None of them guarantees instant success. Success in implementing the Habits of Mind will be incremental and sequential over time, always dependent upon the professional skill of the individual teachers in increasing their capacities and capabilities—developing their intrapersonal intelligence. Equally important is the collaboration with and the synergy of collegial support from other teachers, support staff, administrators, parents, and the students themselves. We suggest starting with the actions listed in Figure 4.1; they also serve as the structure of this chapter.

FIGURE 4.1

Suggested Actions for Implementing Habits of Mind

- Determine what skills and processes students need to know.
- Choose a big idea to steer student success by.
- Develop a nurturing culture.
- Raise Habits of Mind to the consciousness level.
- Talk the talk; use the vocabulary.
- Position the teacher as collegial learner.
- Use thinking time to maintain focus.
- Seek school management support.
- Integrate the habits directly into curriculum and instruction.
- Relate new ideas to what is already known.
- Know where you are and where to go next.
- Use teachable moments positively.
- Know what is happening.

Determine What Skills and Processes Students Need to Know

Recently Alan was asked, "What skills do our students need for the world into which they will go?" His answer was this:

> We don't know exactly what sort of world they are going to have to cope with. There will be paradox; there will be situations when the answers are not known, requiring new and previously unknown solutions; and there will be a need for lifelong learning. Unfortunately we don't know what the paradoxes will be, we do not know what the situations are for which the answers will not be known, and we don't know what it is that we will have to learn, unlearn, or relearn.
>
> What we do know is that we need to produce efficacious, "can do" people who are confident but not brash: people who are all-rounders, alive, outgoing, and friendly; people prepared to give it a go with an awareness of why they are doing it and how best to do it; above all, people with the ability to think!

Traditional schooling based on a largely academic curriculum simply cannot provide what is needed if it is only about blindly *doing*. Doing without understanding is sterile. It leads to thinking that is mechanically correct but patently wrong. Thus Wiggins and McTighe (1998) are able to quote an instance in which an 8th grade national test asked how many buses the army needs to transport 1,128 soldiers if each bus holds 36 soldiers. Almost one third of the students answered correctly but blindly—31, remainder 12!

Carol Dweck's (2006) work is relevant here. She emphasizes the importance of *process* as well as results. She found that students who were focused solely on results when they came upon a difficulty thought they were not intelligent enough to get the answer and so gave up. Those who focused on the process persisted.

Implementing the Habits of Mind into the classroom and into the school culture introduces a series of processes not only important in their own right, but also flexible enough to form important links with other concepts and processes.

Choose a Big Idea to Steer By

The right activities and processes do not just happen. They have to be planned. Moreover, because our core activity is education, what happens in classrooms needs that focus. Thus, our first priority is to know what our educational goals are. We believe that the overarching goal is to teach the curriculum in such a way that students will have the skills needed for them to behave intelligently when they are faced with problems for which the answer is not immediately known—the skills embodied in the Habits of Mind. Such a big idea has relevance well beyond the classroom, providing first the student and later the adult with the skills to tackle the twin problems of paradox and uncertainty in a more and more complex world. Such a goal will also provide students with the skills to become independent thinkers and learners and thus prepare them to be true *lifelong* learners.

Develop a Nurturing Culture

Big ideas are fine, but unless they have a culture in which to grow, they will wither and die, perhaps even be stillborn. A nurturing culture is one that is open to many ideas and possibilities, but not in the sense of "anything goes." The role the teacher takes on is crucial. Teachers must still be in charge, still take responsibility for the quality of curriculum delivery, and for providing a physically and emotionally safe and disciplined work environment; but they must do this more as a collegial facilitator than as an autocratic dictator. Teachers need to be *doing with* students rather than *dealing to* them.

Georgette uses posters illustrating the various Habits of Mind as a physical part of this culture. By placing these on her classroom walls, she is both providing her students with a colorful visual reference to the Habits of Mind and laying the foundation for later activation of episodic memory. Wherever they are in the future, students may recall the habits by thinking of the posters. Beyond that, the posters contribute to the "critical mass" being developed to raise students' consciousness of the Habits of Mind (as described in the next section); they become a visual part of the habits' collective impact, part of the movement toward attainment of the big idea.

To address the preferences of kinesthetic or tactile learners in the class, movement should be part of the classroom culture. For example, students should be allowed to move from their desks to a poster on the wall to read it if that particular habit is being focused on, or perhaps just to have an opportunity for movement and touch. The walk will activate the kinesthetic learners' ability to concentrate. Tactile learners, as they read or simply look at the posters, will also be better able to concentrate by touching or even rubbing with their fingers the carpet-type covering that many schools now have on their walls. Inclusive actions and activities such as these do much to promote a nourishing culture.

Raise Habits of Mind to the Consciousness Level

Students and their teachers need to consciously understand how the Habits of Mind are developing their thinking processes. Unless the students and their teacher are able to understand and articulate their individual capabilities and capacities, they will not have the conscious skills to overcome problems of paradox or uncertainty, or to solve problems for which the answer is not known. Self-awareness is crucial to effectively self-manage and manage relationships with others. Consciousness of the Habits of Mind is a developmental process that takes time. There is no quick fix, no silver bullet.

Talk the Talk, Use the Vocabulary

Talking the talk informally and at every opportunity is one of a series of ongoing, all-encompassing processes for raising Habits of Mind to the consciousness level. Over time, simply using the vocabulary of the Habits of Mind develops a common shared language within the learning community, whether that community is the classroom, the school, or the wider parent and community group. The vocabulary does need to use kid-friendly or parent-friendly language, but without being fluffy or vague, thus ensuring *precision and accuracy*. Talking the talk and using the vocabulary help to develop the verbal linguistic intelligence that is stored in the semantic memory's storage system ready for retrieval later. As this talking the talk progresses, this verbal store grows from the fluffiness that characterizes the unconsciously incompetent stage of the novice to the precision and clarity that characterize the unconscious competence of the expert. As both student and teacher articulate their experiences, a richness of language and metaphor develops.

Because language is the vehicle through which we think, this richness then provides for the development of greater depth and breadth of understanding and practice. This development leads to a comfortable familiarity, which in turn leads to confidence, which enables the emotional memory to be working in a positive way. Thus the student and teacher feel safe—and therefore *responsible risk taking* becomes an option.

Position the Teacher as Collegial Learner

Talking the talk in a collegial way is a delicate process. The teacher, even an experienced teacher, is as much a learner as the student and is to some extent a novice—maybe even unconsciously incompetent! At the same time, however, the teacher is responsible for making the learning environment safe. The classroom's nurturing culture, mentioned earlier, must be a collegial one. The students are the fish; the classroom is the sea. If the sea is not kept at the right temperature, the fish will die. The classroom culture thus has two sides: it needs to signify a sense of order and security, but it also needs to signify a relaxed flexibility that encourages experimentation and creative innovation—an openness to *continuous learning* by the teacher as well as the students. In multiple intelligence terms, such openness means a desire to grow the personal intelligences.

The teacher must still be in control, but as a respected mentor of the students rather than as a social friend or an autocratic despot. This relationship is the "doing with" that Alfie Kohn (1996) advocates. Such a relationship has a profound impact on the students' willingness to accept feedback, which is so effective in lifting student performance. It removes the opportunity to see the feedback as a threat and therefore to shut the feedback out and fight, flee, or freeze.

As their ability to talk the talk and accept and give feedback grows, both the teacher's and the students' capacities and capabilities are increased. Furthermore, the increases will not be limited to just these aspects. The importance of these actions is that they contribute to the growth of the intrapersonal and interpersonal intelligences of both teacher and students. The concept of teacher as learner must never be lost sight of. Teachers must practice the Habits of Mind, too.

Use Thinking Time to Maintain Focus

Talking the talk informally, as suggested in the earlier sections, is important. But as important as it is, this activity can easily lack focus. A more formal process is needed to keep the focus. The idea of thinking time, which comes from Mary Budd Rowe's (1986) observation of teachers' questioning, fits perfectly here as a process to maintain focus.

Thinking time has several significant aspects (see Figure 4.2). First, there is the use of a distinct pause at every stage of questioning: the pause after asking a question, a further pause before calling on a student to respond to the question, another pause before calling on another student to reflect on the answer, and so on through the entire process. Second, those students called on to reflect on what a previous student has said must start by concisely paraphrasing the previous speaker's talk. Third, the teacher avoids becoming involved unless a summary is required at the

FIGURE 4.2

Thinking Time

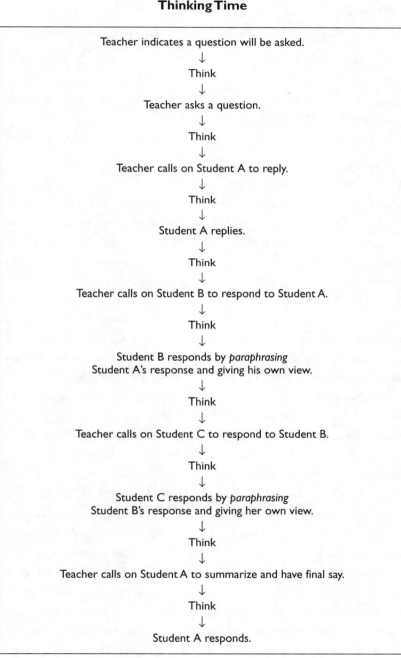

Teacher indicates a question will be asked.
↓
Think
↓
Teacher asks a question.
↓
Think
↓
Teacher calls on Student A to reply.
↓
Think
↓
Student A replies.
↓
Think
↓
Teacher calls on Student B to respond to Student A.
↓
Think
↓
Student B responds by *paraphrasing*
Student A's response and giving his own view.
↓
Think
↓
Teacher calls on Student C to respond to Student B.
↓
Think
↓
Student C responds by *paraphrasing*
Student B's response and giving her own view.
↓
Think
↓
Teacher calls on Student A to summarize and have final say.
↓
Think
↓
Student A responds.

end, or a prompt is needed to allow the student to be more detailed or articulate.

Thinking time uses three rules:

1. After the question is asked, no one raises his or her hand until called upon to answer.

2. Before responding to the previous speaker, the responding student paraphrases the previous student's comments.

3. Teacher comment is saved for the end and is given only if necessary.

These rules keep students engaged and actively listening. No one knows who is going to be called on to answer, and therefore the students cannot relax and disengage on the assumption that those with their hands up will be asked and the others will not. All must be prepared. All must concentrate on what is being said in order to be able to paraphrase correctly rather than be disengaged because they are thinking about what their answer will be or daydreaming.

The silence—the pauses—of thinking time allows for *listening with empathy*, for the accessing of *past knowledge*, for *reflection*, and for formulating a response with *precision and accuracy*. The research shows that provided the pause is at least three seconds long or perhaps considerably longer for more complex, higher-level questioning, several results occur: responses change from single words to whole statements; guessing, statements of "I don't know," and inappropriate responses decrease; self-confidence increases; responses by slower learners increase; speculative thinking increases; students piggyback on each other's responses; interaction becomes a student–student discussion moderated by the teacher rather than a teacher–student inquisition; students ask more questions; both teacher and student are more likely to use Bloom's higher-level thinking skills; and finally—the important bottom line—achievement improves. In summary, not only does discipline improve, but also expectancy rises for all; and once the culture is one of success, accelerated learning follows.

Thinking time is also an ideal process for more formal *metacognitive reflection* and discussion. It is relatively easy to plan for discussion time on whatever habit or habits the class is focusing on, whether it is to correct a fault or to develop expertise. The teacher will gain greater *precision and accuracy* about each student's progress, especially where students are required to respond randomly.

Seek School Management Support

Principals and those in senior management positions have an important role in implementing the Habits of Mind. Alan made a point of introducing Habits of Mind terminology and anecdotes into his school assembly talks and in the notices that he was required to provide for both staff and students. Staff meetings, newsletters, and notices to parents were another avenue for talking the talk and using the vocabulary. The communication provided an opportunity to model *precision and accuracy*. The information to students had to be in kid-friendly language; the information to staff, in teacher-friendly language; and the information to parents, in parent-friendly language. The use of three different kinds of language modeled *flexibility*. But more important, Habits of Mind talk was integrated into the management processes. It was lived.

At least in qualitative terms, we need to gather schoolwide evidence of student and teacher acquisition and practice in the use of Habits of Mind and how that affects academic and social achievement. Alan gathered evidence by requiring writing assignments based on students' metacognition to be part of the classroom routine and thus was included in the classroom and school culture. The writing assignment sometimes occurs at the end of a unit; sometimes at the end of the week. In any case, the writing was done regularly and provided further evidence of the big idea being achieved.

The excerpt that follows shows an example of the students' metacognitive writing. The Year 8 students (12-year-olds) had been given the task from time to time to team up as mentors with the new-entrant emergent writers (the 5-year-olds) to scribe for them, because the younger students could not yet write themselves. The excerpt is a student's metacognitive reflection on one such experience. The writing provided the evidence we needed to confirm we were on track. Habits of Mind had been new to this student when the year started. The metacognitive reflection was written two-thirds of the way through the year.

I was impressed by the amount of things these little kids know, but I also had to use a lot of *listening with empathy* as they were very quiet. I had to use a lot of *flexibility* in my thinking, as some things they said did not fully make sense. Our group had to be very *persistent* with our little one as she gave up easy. We had to use a lot of *clarity* in our language, as she was only little. We also had to *manage a lot of impulsivity* by not telling Laura the answers. We had to do a lot of *questioning* to get her on the right track. I really enjoyed helping this child. I hope it helped her a lot. I also had to check for a lot of *accuracy* and make sure I was writing down what she told me. I think it's a great idea to help little children like that.

Integrate Habits of Mind Directly into Curriculum and Instruction

If the Habits of Mind are to be an important part of the culture of the school, there needs to be a process for them to be explicitly integrated into the delivery of the curriculum and used in every lesson and in every activity. If students are not aware of the habits, their ability to become independent, lifelong learners is compromised and stunted—even prevented.

Georgette's study of the arctic tern is an example of how this integration is done and shows how the habits can be highlighted both in subject matter content and in delivery of instruction. The arctic tern is a small seabird that has earned the reputation of being the champion of migratory birds. Each year it makes a journey of 21,700 miles (35,000 kilometers)—roughly the circumference of the earth. To make this journey, the arctic tern requires committed *persistence* because the loss of even a day could put it behind schedule and cause it to die. To maintain its *persistence*, the tern breaks down its long journey by pacing itself. This pacing allows even a young bird to cover enormous distances. One such bird tagged in the Arctic Circle (the terns' breeding ground) was found 11,000 miles (17,600 kilometers) south less than three months later.

To ensure that the lesson on the arctic tern would have *clarity and precision*, Georgette devised a flowchart that gave both her and her students a clear and precise visual overview of the lesson (see Figure 4.3).

FIGURE 4.3

Example of How Habits of Mind Relate to Lesson Content and Instruction

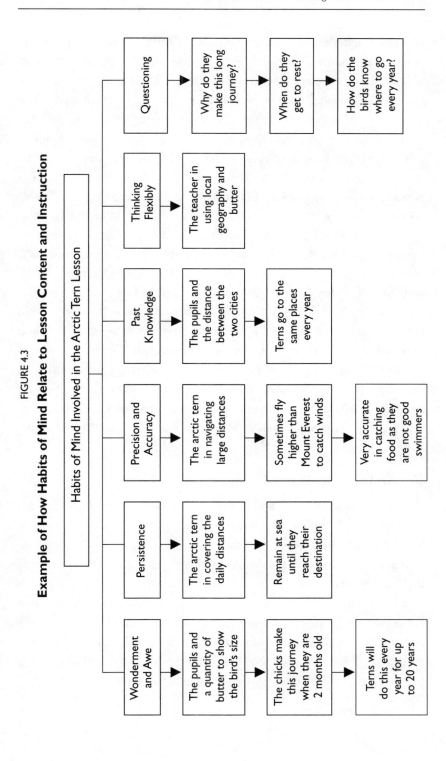

Habits of Mind Involved in the Arctic Tern Lesson

Wonderment and Awe	Persistence	Precision and Accuracy	Past Knowledge	Thinking Flexibly	Questioning
The pupils and a quantity of butter to show the bird's size	The arctic tern in covering the daily distances	The arctic tern in navigating large distances	The pupils and the distance between the two cities	The teacher in using local geography and butter	Why do they make this long journey?
The chicks make this journey when they are 2 months old	Remain at sea until they reach their destination	Sometimes fly higher than Mount Everest to catch winds	Terns go to the same places every year		When do they get to rest?
Terns will do this every year for up to 20 years		Very accurate in catching food as they are not good swimmers			How do the birds know where to go every year?

The teacher's role as a learner and a manager is clearly shown in the flowchart. Gardner (1999) defines *intrapersonal intelligence* as the possession of "an effective model of oneself—including one's own desires, fears, and capacities" (p. 43). For a teacher, that means having an efficacious, "can do" approach. Habits of Mind are among those capacities that allow a teacher to be efficacious. Georgette had the capacity to produce a flowchart that showed with *clarity and precision* the major points in the lesson and thus provided focus. Moreover, in so doing she was applying *past knowledge* (her previous use of thinking maps) and *thinking flexibly* about how to apply that *past knowledge* in a new and different context.

Likewise, *interpersonal* intelligence is defined as "a person's capacity to understand the intentions, motivations, and desires of other people and, consequently to work effectively with others" (Gardner, 1999, p. 43). Georgette used this intelligence when she produced the flowchart and continued beyond that when she thought *flexibly* and made the connection between the tern's flight and the personal knowledge of the students. Such personal connections are essential for real mastery (Caine et al., 2005).

Both of us believe that it is important for teachers to be conscious that concepts such as Gardner's multiple intelligences are for students and teachers. As teachers gain personal, practical knowledge through their mindful application of Habits of Mind, their personal intelligences grow as well.

Relate Ideas to What Is Already Known

What teachers understand and do is at least as important as what students know and do. To truly understand the journey of the tern and the *persistence* involved in its journey, the teacher needed to convey this in as authentic a manner as possible. To accomplish this, the distance of the tern's daily flight was broken down and then related to the students' own geographical area—to what the students currently knew. In this case, it was the distance between their home city, Gisborne, on the east coast of New Zealand's North Island, and another east coast city farther south, Napier. Thus the *persistence* of the tern was related to the students' *prior knowledge*, which in turn provided the students with meaningful understanding.

Meaningfulness was further developed when Georgette took a 500-gram package of butter (about 17½ ounces, or just over one pound) and cut away 200 grams, leaving 300 grams (about two-thirds of a pound) — the weight of the bird. This 300-gram piece was then placed on the palm of the student's hand. Understanding the actual weight of the bird — it was not big and powerful — coupled with understanding the distance traveled brought home the reality of the bird's accomplishment, and thus opened up the students to responding with *wonderment and awe*.

The lesson about the Arctic tern shows a developing *interdependence*. Although we normally tend to think of *thinking interdependently* as working with others in a synergistic way, it can be extended to include the *interdependence* between the various Habits of Mind, too. There is strength and a synergy in being so aware of these connections that then increase the breadth and depth of students' capabilities and capacities.

Know Where You Are and Where to Go Next

In developing the Habits of Mind or any other skill, it is helpful to have a sense of where you are currently and what the next steps are to achieve the ultimate goal of mastery. Rubrics can help provide this information. The effectiveness of rubrics is well supported by research showing considerable percentage-point gains in student achievement when they are used correctly. They provide a clear idea of the ultimate target and the steps to reach it. There are a number of ways to construct rubrics. However, rubrics are likely to be most effective when they are constructed with student input, thus giving ownership and control. *Interdependence* again.

Georgette regularly uses a process based on brainstorming. If she wants her class to improve their *precision and accuracy*, she has the class brainstorm ideas about *precision and accuracy*. After that she has her students use the higher-level thinking skill of analysis to categorize and consolidate the brainstorm ideas, and finally she places the ideas in a hierarchy using the Dreyfus and Dreyfus (1986) novice-to-expert terminology.

Secondary school music specialist Mary Stubbings varies this rubric construction with an approach based on the multiple intelligences. Her class looks at each intelligence and brainstorms how they fit into the unit

FIGURE 4.4

Metacognition by Dialogue

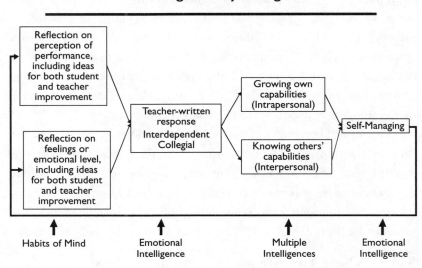

of work. The activity highlights in particular the capacities and capabilities that the student will require to complete the task. Thus the students not only know what strengths they bring to the work and how these can enhance their work, but they also know what strengths and capabilities they need to develop to achieve an even better result. Such an approach also demonstrates a positive, integrated approach rather than a deficit ("I can only do it this way") model.

Some years ago Georgette developed a system whereby she responded in writing to the weekly metacognition pieces written by the students. This system, now called *metacognition by dialogue*, is illustrated in Figure 4.4. The technique was singled out in a report by researchers at Massey University in New Zealand (Ball, Vossler, Gibbs, & Broadley, 1999) for its effectiveness and for being a vehicle for students to reflect, self-analyze, and make recommendations about how to improve their performance.

Alan has been working one-on-one with a 15-year-old girl on time management. She, like many other adolescents, had developed the habit of leaving her project assignments undone until the last minute and

underachieving. An approach using a rubric was chosen. The first decision was about where she wanted to be. That is, she needed to decide on
her "big idea." She decided that she simply wanted to "complete a perfect
assignment." In this case that decision was fine, but in a normal classroom
situation where the rubric is designed to set a pattern for attaining the
curriculum goal or a standard, the teacher may well need to provide this
expert target.

The next step required was an honest appraisal of where she was right
then—the current situation. This was expressed as putting things off
because she had other things to do and ending up in a crisis mode. At this
stage, Covey's (1994) quadrant was introduced to give some structure to
her understanding of what was happening, and what should be happening instead. This showed her operating almost exclusively in the time
wasting third and fourth quadrants: the urgent but not important that is
temporary and fleeting, and the not urgent or important trivia such as gos-
siping with school friends or texting them on her cell phone, thus squan-
dering her time. This then led her to become trapped in the first quadrant
when the importance and urgency of the assignment deadline loomed,
forcing her into crisis management where all that mattered was to complete her assignment regardless of quality and without time for reflection
or revision. What she needed to do was to move into the second quadrant where she could proactively operate to give herself time to reflect
and revise, thus eventually completing the perfect assignment. Following
that, all that was required was to brainstorm in order to fill in the criteria
for the development stages that would culminate in the expert producing
a perfect assignment.

Finally, two columns were added to the rubric. One was for what
would be seen at each level, and the other was for what would be heard
or said at each level. This structure not only gave specific criteria for assessing the level, but it also related it back to the practical things she needed
to do to achieve her big picture—the perfect assignment.

The wording of the rubric had to be in her words—the right words for
her—so that she had ownership. It had to speak to her rather than to Alan
or to some preconceived idea of correctness. Thus although verbal linguistic intelligence was important, it was less a grammatical correctness

FIGURE 4.5

Excerpt from Student-Teacher E-Mail Dialogue

Student's Metacognition	Teacher's Response
This week I did not do much homework until today. This shows that my transition from novice to apprentice is still in progress as I left it to the last minute. However, I did do the planning on paper rather than in my brain so that is definitely an apprentice characteristic. Unfortunately, the procrastination that happened this weekend is not. I found myself floating into the fourth box of Covey, doing things that were both unnecessary and not urgent. To avoid this in future I am going to actively write down what I need to achieve so I can cross it off as I go along, and if I need to switch activities (because I can't concentrate on what I am doing because I have been doing it for awhile) I can flip between the tasks on my list above my desk. This has worked previously and I am going to try it over the next week.	The reference to the rubric is the right way to look at what you are doing. For next week start off with a paragraph saying exactly why you put it all off to the end; i.e., what were the Quadrant 4 things that you were doing? Then state a way or ways you can control this. You might still want/ need to do some of these things, so it may be a case of control rather than cutting out completely. Habits of Mind are very important because we think and work in patterns. One of the H of M is *applying past knowledge*, and this is what is happening here as you say, "this has worked previously." There are 16 habits in all, and you are working here with *metacognition/reflection* as you think carefully about what you are doing; and there is also *precision and accuracy* in that you're working toward getting your homework and assignment study patterns right, as you show by reference to the rubric. In doing this you are *persisting* too, which is working things out so you can accomplish something and not giving up or doing the same old thing over and over. *Flexibility in thinking* is the way you seek solutions to your study needs by looking for better alternatives and almost certainly *managing impulsivity* as you grapple with those Quadrant 4 distractions.

or even *precision of meaning* that was important, but more an *emotional precision* that she felt comfortable with. There needed to be "sensitivity" (Gardner, 1999).

Figure 4.5 is an extract from the weekly e-mail dialogue between Alan and the student. Her metacognition shows that she is self-analyzing in some detail and that this is aided by the rubric, which she uses as a reference point. This self-analysis then gives her the information needed to evaluate where she is and what she needs to plan and do for herself in order to move to the next level on the rubric. Thus she is operating at the three top levels of the new Bloom thinking hierarchy: analyze, evaluate, create.

Note, too, that Alan's dialogue with her is in a conversational tone that is positive and constructive. He builds on what she has started, and although the voice of authority is present, it is more of a collegial level than a command-and-control level. He also tries to be helpful by defining any terms used, such as the Habits of Mind vocabulary, and relating them to her area of experience and understanding. This approach aims to ensure that there is personal meaning for her.

Use Teachable Moments Positively

Apart from the ordinary day-to-day flow of classroom activity, the teacher needs to be on the lookout for extraordinary events to use for "talking the talk," and once having spotted them, to be flexible enough to reap the benefit from them. Middle school teacher Andrea Niven did exactly that. She had Georgette's posters on her walls when the following events, described in her journal, took place:

> We have all the Habit of Mind posters displayed—which I at first thought may detract from the one we are focusing on, but I have found at least at this stage that it is great to be able to refer to them when appropriate, especially those we may not have time to cover with any depth. *HUMOR* is the one I am thinking of specifically. We have been having drug education sessions with Life Ed. The presenter has an accent, which he apologized for in advance, regarding mispronunciation of names. A group of my boys thought it was hilarious when one of the girl's names was mispronounced—the ensuing giggling meant they were highly unlikely to get the messages that were being delivered. Fortunately, it was towards the end of the session. On returning to class, we looked quickly at *HUMOR* and then talked about the age of the baby in the television program *Ice-Age*, and the kind of things that made her laugh (people getting hurt, etc.). We decided that

this probably reflected *immature humor,* and then talked about what kind of humor laughing AT other people was. A few sheepish looks from a few sheepish boys and I knew my point was made. Further mispronunciations at our next session, and not a titter to be heard. The presenter has commented to the class that they show a maturity beyond that shown by other groups he has worked with, especially regarding their questions and their ability to cope with more advanced information.

Andrea's experience is a great example of the teachable moment—being able to take advantage of a situation, not being constrained by the lesson plan for the day, and turning a negative incident into a positive one. In Habit of Mind terms, it shows the teacher both *taking responsible risks* and *thinking flexibly* as she seized the teachable moment and used it effectively. It also showed the teacher to have intrapersonal and interpersonal intelligences to enable her to think efficaciously and therefore be able to make a difference. Those two intelligences were in turn further strengthened for both teacher and student by the practical personal knowledge the whole series of events produced. The inference is that the students' higher-level thinking skills kicked in, as evidenced by the presenter's comments regarding the maturity of the questions asked. And furthermore, within this small series of events are the attributes of Goleman's (1995) emotional intelligence. There were at least two of the self-management skills he highlights, self-awareness and self-regulation, as the students became aware of the implications of laughing *at* someone or something, and as a result were now able to manage relationships, as was shown in the follow-up lesson.

Know What Is Happening

We believe in the teacher and student working in a collegial, mentor-type relationship in which both are learners. We believe in the integration and inclusion of as wide a variety of practices as possible. We believe in both student and teacher being reflective practitioners. The more strands, the more synapse strengtheners there are. The stronger the synapses, the more the teaching and learning will be remembered. The more strands, the greater the opportunity for individual learners to have their needs met. However, all these elements lose traction, lose any real impact unless they are brought to the consciousness level. Both student and teacher must know and understand what is happening if either is to reach his potential. The more detail they each have about how they learn, the more they have the knowledge to improve their ability to learn. The more they are able to improve their ability to learn, the better able they are to become successful lifelong learners willing and able to face challenge and even paradox.

References

Ball, T., Vossler, K., Gibbs, C., & Broadley, G. (1999). *St. George's School: Teaching thinking: An evaluation of the process involved in innovative curriculum development.* Unpublished research report. College of Education, Massey University, Palmerston North, New Zealand.

Caine, R. N., Caine, G., McClintic, C., & Klimek, K. (2008). *12 brain/mind learning principles in action: Developing executive functions of the human brain,* (2nd ed.) Thousand Oaks, CA: Corwin.

Covey, S. R. (1994). *The seven habits of highly effective people.* Melbourne, Australia: Simon & Schuster.

Dreyfus, H. L., & Dreyfus, S. E. (1986). *Mind over machine.* New York: Free Press.

Dweck, C. (2006). *Mindset.* New York: Random House.

Gardner, H. (1999). *Intelligence reframed.* New York: Basic Books.

Goleman, D. (1995). *Emotional intelligence.* London: Bloomsbury Publishing.

Kohn, A. (1996). What to look for in classrooms. *Education Leadership,* 54(1), 54–55.

Rowe, M. B. (1986). Wait-time: Slowing down may be a way of speeding up. *Journal of Teacher Education,* 37(1), 43–50.

Wiggins, G., & McTighe, J. (1998). *Understanding by design.* Alexandria, VA: ASCD.

5

Teaching Habits of Mind

Arthur L. Costa and Bena Kallick

A great pleasure in life is doing what people say you cannot do.
—*Tommy John*

The Habits of Mind don't readily lend themselves to instructional "recipes." Still, many educators have developed strategies for teaching the Habits of Mind directly, from building students' awareness of them to instructing children specifically on each habit. These educators share some of their strategies in this chapter. Though their processes and methods differ, all of their work has a common strain: effective teachers are always alert for and seize opportunities to engage, reinforce, illuminate, and practice the Habits of Mind.

Building Awareness

Many teachers build students' awareness of the Habits of Mind through the questions they pose. For example, before you begin a learning activity, ask questions that cue students about and focus their attention on the importance and use of one or more of the habits. For example, you might ask questions such as these:

• "As you anticipate your projects, which of the Habits of Mind might you need to use?"

- "In working these math problems, which of the Habits of Mind will help us?"
- "As we read, which of the Habits of Mind will we use to help us understand the story?"

After a learning activity, you might pose questions that lead to reflection on and synthesis of the Habits of Mind:

- "As you reflect on your work on this project, which of the Habits of Mind did you find yourself using?"
- "As you solved these problems, which of the Habits of Mind did you use?"
- "As you worked in groups to design a plan, what metacognitive strategies did you use to monitor your performance of the Habits of Mind?"

Well-constructed questions also cue students to transfer and apply the Habits of Mind to situations different from those in which the habits were learned. Here are some examples:

- "In what other classes might you use these Habits of Mind?"
- "In what other situations in your life would your use of these Habits of Mind be beneficial?"
- "In what careers or professions would people have to draw forth these Habits of Mind?"

Other intriguing questions can be posed to stimulate discussion of the Habits of Mind:

- "How might an intelligent person use the Habits of Mind to choose a doctor?"
- "How would the Habits of Mind be used in purchasing an automobile?"
- "Which of the Habits of Mind would be helpful in intelligently reading a newspaper (or watching television)?"

Teaching the Habits Directly

Many teachers have developed powerful strategies for teaching the Habits of Mind directly. Though some of these strategies focus on one habit, other habits are often interdependently linked to them. In fact, clusters of habits can be taught, depending on student needs, the context and content of the lesson, and the school's educational priorities.

The following examples are drawn from many different classrooms. We have tried to provide some rich exemplars for you to use as a model for your own teaching. You will, of course, want to draw on your own skills and repertoire and add to this list.

Persisting

If the only tool you have is a hammer, you will treat the whole world as if it were a nail.

—*Edward de Bono*

When students approach a problem, they often have the misconception that there is "one best strategy." If that strategy does not work, they give up in frustration. People persist because they can draw on multiple ways to solve problems. If Plan A doesn't work, they back up and try Plan B. Therefore, teachers must celebrate multiple ways of finding solutions: "Isn't that wonderful! We've found four different ways of solving this problem!" As students build their repertoire of strategies, they also begin to see the merit of working with other students.

It is better to teach students three ways to solve one problem than it is to teach them one way to solve three problems. We've seen many teachers who are in the habit of asking, "Who has another way to solve this problem?" "What is another approach to solving this problem?" or "What are some other strategies?" They then ask students to write about their many different strategies for a "strategy box." When students are in doubt about another problem, they can refer to their strategy box. Figure 5.1 shows how letter writing can be a useful way for students to reflect on the Habits of Mind and learn to manage their impulsivity.

Teaching persistence is a matter of teaching strategy. Persistence does not just mean working to get it right. Persistence means knowing that getting stuck is a cue to "try something else."

Managing Impulsivity

The secret of getting ahead is getting started. The secret of getting started is breaking your complex overwhelming tasks into small manageable tasks, and then starting on the first one.

—*Mark Twain*

Before any learning activity, teachers must take the time to develop and discuss strategies for attacking problems. Such work should include rules, directions, time constraints, and purposes. Students can use this guidance during their work and to evaluate their performance afterward.

During an activity, teachers should invite students to share their progress, thought processes, and perceptions of their own behavior. Guide students through metacognition by asking them to describe where they are in using a particular strategy and to reflect on how well that strategy is working. At this time, it is also useful to ask students to map their progress visually. They can describe the trail of thinking to this point in their work. Then they can describe the paths they intend to pursue next to solve their problem.

FIGURE 5.1

A 3rd Grader's Reflections on the Habits of Mind

Dear Ms. —

Hello.... We were estima-
ting the cost of our school supplies. Then we calculated the prices
of the supplies. The cost of everything
together was nineteen sixty [$19.60]. Most
of the groups got different numbers for
the estimates.

I used intelligent behaviors [hab-
its of mind]. The first one I used was
persistence. The second one I used
was prior knowledge. I used persistence because I needed to keep trying
to get the right answer. I used
prior knowledge because I had to
use what I know about money.
That's all I have to say.

Sincerely,

(Student)

This kind of visual map also serves as a diagnostic cognitive map of student thinking, which the teacher can use to give more individualized assistance. If students are using a time management plan, this is a good point for them to review and revise their plan. This also is an excellent time to provide students with peer coaching or to introduce the concept of a critical friend (Costa & Kallick, 1995).

Once the learning activity is completed, teachers can invite students to evaluate how they worked with the rules, strategies, and instructions. Students can use this reflection to generate alternative, more efficient strategies to use in the future.

We know a kindergarten teacher who begins and ends each day with a class meeting. In the morning, children plan for the day. They decide what learning tasks to accomplish and how to accomplish them. They allocate classroom space, assign roles, and develop criteria for appropriate conduct. Throughout the day, the teacher calls attention to plans and ground rules established during the morning. The teacher also invites students to compare what they are doing with what was agreed to. Then, before dismissal, students hold another class meeting to reflect on, evaluate, and plan further strategies and criteria.

Wait time is another important element in learning to manage impulsivity. When using wait time, teachers will want to share with students why they ask questions and then remain silent. Tell children that you are looking for thoughtful, reflective answers and you will wait a minute or so before calling on anyone. Let them know you are not looking for how quickly someone answers a question, and you will not be impressed with answers that are shouted out or hands that shoot up before the question is completed.

In one school, everyone was working on the goal of using wait time. The principal stopped a student running down the hallway, pulled out a stopwatch, and showed the student the timing of one minute. Then the principal asked, "Can you tell me why you were running?" Stopwatches, egg timers, and other timing devices help students learn how to wait appropriately.

Listening with Understanding and Empathy

Nothing increases the respect and gratitude of one man for another more than when he is heard exactly and with interest.

—R. Umbach

I understand that when I'm reading a question I listen for key words to help me go about understanding the question and help me answer it.

—Friendship Valley Student Self-Assessment
Friendship Valley Elementary School
Carroll County, Maryland

We spend about 55 percent of our lives listening, but listening is one of the least taught skills in schools. Adults often say they are listening when actually they are rehearsing in their heads what they will say when it's their turn to speak. We need to teach students the skills of listening: pausing, paraphrasing, questioning, and taking turns talking.

Effective listeners set aside certain unproductive mental patterns that may block their capacity to listen. According to Richard Bommelje (www.listeningleaders.com), when we listen, we often are fighting the urge to do one of several things:

• Compare. When our mind compares, we are distracted from listening because we try to assess who is smarter, more competent, or more resourceful.

• Read minds. When we read minds, we try to figure out what the other person really is thinking and feeling. We don't pay much attention to what that person is actually saying.

• Rehearse. When our attention is on preparing and crafting our next comment, we don't take time to listen.

• Filter. When we listen to some things and not to others, we pay attention only to those ideas with which we agree or disagree.

• Judge. The negative labels we hold about others or their ideas prejudice our listening. We don't pay as much attention to what they say because we've already decided they are unqualified or unworthy.

• Dream. When we are only half-listening, something the person says suddenly triggers a chain of private associations. Then we're off and running in our own fantasy world.

• Identify. Autobiographical thinking blocks our listening because we relate what the other person says to our own experience. For example, a friend describes a visit to the automobile repair shop, which reminds us of our car's most recent breakdown.

• Give advice. Because we view ourselves as great problem solvers, ready with help and eager to give suggestions, we immediately begin searching for the right solution to the other person's problem.

• Argue. When we argue, counter, or debate, other people may feel that they've not been heard because we're so quick to disagree.

• Be right. Because our mind is made up, we twist facts, raise our voice, make excuses, accuse others, or call up past sins to avoid being wrong.

• Derail. When we are bored or uncomfortable with the topic, we change the subject or deflect the conversation to another issue.

• Placate. Because we want to be amiable and have people like us, we agree with everything to avoid confrontation.

• Scrutinize. Asking repeated, probing questions drags the conversation into a hole of analytical minutiae and may cause others to lose sight of larger issues.

To practice the skills of listening, ask students to paraphrase what another student has said before they add to what was said or offer their own comments. Invite students to describe what goes on in their heads as they listen. For example, you might ask, "As your partner was speaking, what metacognitive processes did you use to manage, monitor, and modify your listening capacities when you had an urge to . . . ?" Figure 5.2 shows a poster one teacher at Friendship Valley Elementary School in Westminster, Maryland, uses to remind her students of good listening habits.

FIGURE 5.2
Listening Poster

Strategies for Students to Manage Distractors to Listening

Before I start to think:

- **What are my distractions?**
- **What will I do to stay focused?**

Distraction: Anything that pulls your attention from what you should be doing—listening, reading, writing, and sharing

Class Brainstorming of Distractions

What I see or hear:

- **Pictures on the wall**
- **Noises in the hall**
- **Children talking**
- **Teachers talking**
- **Lawn mower outside**
- **Noises in the classroom**
- **Chairs moving**
- **Books**

The room may be:

Too hot	*Too cold*	*Can't see*	*Too sunny*
Too noisy	*Can't hear*	*Too many things going on*	

Source: Teacher at Friendship Valley Elementary School, Carroll County, Maryland.

Thinking Flexibly

> We need people who can read and write. But what we really need
> is people who cannot only read the instructions but change them.
> They need to be able to think outside the lines.
>
> —*Richard Gurin, CEO and President*
> *Binney & Smith Crayola Products*

We enhance the habit of thinking flexibly when we must alter our perspective and see things from other points of view. *Macrocentric* thinking
means seeing the big picture. *Microcentric* thinking means finding the
details. *Retrocentric* thinking means starting with the end point and working backward toward the beginning. To help students understand these
different perspectives, have them read stories such as *The True Story of
the Three Little Pigs from the Wolf's Point of View* or Chris Van Allsburg's
Two Bad Ants. Deliberately place students in heterogeneous groups based
on their different learning styles, which will help them understand and
appreciate varying points of view. Create a problem-solving team with students who have visual strengths and students whose style is auditory. Ask
them to explain to each other how to solve a problem "outside" their best
learning style.

You can take this approach even further by giving students problems
in which they have to change their perspective to find an answer. Have
them describe how they had to look at the problem differently and where
else in life a change in perspective would be important. For example, can
you find the pattern in this string of letters?

AEFHIKLMNTVWXYZ

Thinking About Thinking (Metacognition)

Thinking aloud . . . allowed!

Sometimes teachers are so anxious for students to find correct answers that they omit discussions of the processes, strategies, and steps that produce the answer. Asking students to describe their thinking while they solve a problem seems to beget even more thinking. Students must do more than learn how to find answers; they must become aware of the cognitive processes that produced the answer.

Some teachers ask students to keep a running record of their thought processes as they solve a problem. This record is a powerful teaching tool. It can reveal to you that the student is not accomplishing what was intended because the student is unaware of an unsuccessful strategy. Once you become aware of this problem, you can teach another strategy.

Teachers also use questioning strategies to clarify students' problem-solving processes: "Jeff, you figured out that the answer was 44; Jody says the answer is 33. Let's hear how you came up with 44. Retrace your steps for us." Generating alternative strategies for solving problems and posting them around the room serves two purposes: (1) students are surrounded by multiple possibilities for problem solving when they are stuck, and (2) students see that there is no single best way of doing things.

Clarifying helps students to reexamine their own problem-solving processes, to identify their own errors, and to self-correct. The teacher might ask, "How much is 3 plus 4?"

The student replies, "The answer is 12."

Rather than correct the student, the teacher clarifies: "Gary, how did you arrive at that answer?"

Gary answers, "Well, I multiplied 4 and 3 and got . . . oh, I see! I multiplied instead of added."

By clarifying, the teacher causes students to return to their thinking processes. By restating the processes, students "hear themselves" and become self-correcting.

Teachers also can ask students to identify what they have done well and invite them to seek feedback from their peers. For example, the teacher might ask, "What have you done that you're proud of?" This kind of question helps students become more conscious of their own behavior, and they learn to apply a set of internal criteria for behavior they consider "good" (Costa, 2001).

When students reflect on their learning, teachers can guide that reflection to be metacognitive. Many teachers ask students to solve a problem and then describe their steps to someone else, using these guidelines:

1. What did you do first?
2. What steps did you take when you were uncertain about your work?
3. How did you change your course of action? Was it profitable?
4. If you were to do this work again, is there anything that you would do differently? If so, describe what that might be and why you would do it.

Tell students that answers such as "I can't" or "I don't know how to" are unacceptable. Instead, they should identify what information is required, what materials are needed, or what skills are lacking in order for them to resolve a situation. This reflection helps students identify the boundaries between what they know and what they need to know. Reflection also develops a persevering attitude and enhances the student's ability to create strategies that will produce needed data.

Eventually the processes of thinking and problem solving become the subjects of classroom discussion. Because teachers realize that the intent of metacognitive dialogue is not to arrive at closure, they use techniques and strategies to maintain "opensure"—continuing engagement of the thinking processes. A variety of strategies can help you engage and sustain this metacognition.

When you want students to check for accuracy, ask these questions:

• "How do you know you are right?"
• "What other ways can you prove that you are correct?"

Pause and clarify during your conversation, but don't interrupt:

- "What did you do first?"
- "What clues did you have that you were on the right track?"
- "How did you know where to begin?"
- "What led you to make that decision?"
- "When you said you started at the beginning, how did you know where to begin?"

Provide students with data, but not answers:

- "I think you heard it wrong. Let me repeat the question."
- "You need to check your addition."

Resist making value judgments or agreeing with students' answers:

- "So, your answer is 48. Who came up with a different answer?"
- "That's one possibility. Who solved it another way?"

Stay focused on thinking processes:

- "Tell us what strategies you used to solve the problem."
- "What steps did you take in your solution?"

Invite overt verbalization of thinking processes, and encourage persistence:

- "Tell us what's going on inside your head."
- "C'mon, you can do it! Hang in there."

Striving for Accuracy

It's hard to wring my hands when I am busy rolling up my sleeves.

—*Linda Geraci*

Astronauts use [the Habit of Mind] checking for accuracy before each space mission!

—Student
Friendship Valley Elementary School
Carroll County, Maryland

Students must come to see that striving for accuracy is of great value not only in the classroom but in the wider world as well. Pharmaceutical research, surgery, piloting, bookkeeping—all require a commitment to accuracy. Sometimes teachers take home stacks of student papers to correct, placing ticks and checkmarks to indicate correct or incorrect answers. In this process, teachers get a lot of practice checking for accuracy and precision, but they rob students of the opportunity to check for themselves. Consider this alternative: simply write on the top of the paper, "You have three errors on this page." Now it is the student's responsibility to find and correct the mistakes, not the teacher's.

Another useful strategy is "three before me." No paper should be turned in to the teacher without being checked at least three times. Organize students into teams of four so that they have three other people with whom to share responsibility for striving for accuracy.

Discuss with students the skills and strategies that they might consciously apply when striving for accuracy and precision. Following is a list developed by a 7th grade class and posted in their classroom:

- Always use spell check
- Give your essay or story to a friend for feedback
- Review the rubric to see if you have met the criteria before turning in your paper
- Check your work again and again
- Don't just write the answer—show your work so that you can go back and find errors
- Learn from your mistakes so you won't make them again
- Know the rules and apply them
- Let your paper "sit" for awhile and come back to it with a fresh perspective

- Use a different strategy than the first one (like working a math problem backward) to see if you get the same answer
- Make sure you know what the directions mean before you begin

Questioning and Posing Problems

It is in the formulation of the problem that individuality is expressed, that creativity is stimulated, that nuances and subtleties are discovered.

—Herbert Thelen

Whatever the subject area, it is helpful for students to pose study questions for themselves before and during their reading of textual material. Self-generating questions facilitate comprehension. We know that reading with a purpose stimulates a more focused mind. Questioning while reading provides an opportunity for the reader to predict what is coming next in the story. Many students find it useful to keep their questions in a response log or reading log. Then they can begin to answer the questions raised as they reflect on the reading and seek other sources (see Chapter 12).

Invite students to compose questions to be used in a study guide or on a test. Some teachers ask students to prepare questions in a group to be given to another group. The second group then answers the questions, and the first group evaluates those answers along with the original questions. This activity serves two important purposes. First, students ask more difficult questions because they want to make them hard for the other group. Second, they must be able to answer their own questions, which challenges their own thinking as well.

Sometimes the most significant questions are generated through the research process. There are many ways to guide students to generate powerful questions worthy of research. In addition, students can learn that a thoughtful way to end their research paper is with a set of questions generated as a result of their inquiry. Students gain much when they realize that there is always more to know!

Applying Past Knowledge to New Situations

> The main fuel to speed the world's progress is our stock of knowledge, and the brake is our lack of imagination.
>
> —*Julian Simon*

Teachers must take time to both scaffold and bridge new learning. *Scaffolding* means building a knowledge structure by going back into previous information and drawing it forth. The recalled information then serves as a framework for incorporating new information.

Think of building a new stage in an auditorium. The scaffolds are the structures that hold up the stage as it is being built. Once the structure is complete, however, it is expected to stand on its own, without the scaffolds. Thus it is with learning. Students need scaffolds to support them through new learning. Then they must take the new learning and test its viability as an independent structure. Finally, they must be able to bridge, or transfer, that learning to other situations in their lives inside and outside school.

For example, whenever you begin a new learning, pose questions that will cause students to search their memories to brainstorm and generate past knowledge:

- "What do you remember about . . . ?"
- "When have you ever seen anything like this?"
- "As you recall . . . ."
- "Tell what you already know about . . . ."

When the lesson is over, always ask students to apply their knowledge to the future:

- "If you were to design a new . . . ?"
- "What would it be like if . . . ?"
- "Where else would you use this information?"
- "In what other situations could you apply this?"
- "In what careers and jobs would this Habit of Mind be needed?"

The intent of scaffolding and bridging is to help students get into the habit of drawing forth previous knowledge and applying it to new or novel situations.

Thinking and Communicating with Clarity and Precision

This report, by its very length, defends itself against the risk of being read.

—*Winston Churchill*

Students' and adults' oral language often is filled with omissions, generalizations, and vagueness. Our language is value laden, sometimes deceiving, and conceptual rather than operational (Costa & Marzano, 2001). Being alert to this vagueness and then clarifying or probing for specificity causes others to define their terms, become specific about their actions, make precise comparisons, and use accurate descriptors (Laborde, 1984). Clarifying language also clarifies thoughts.

The vague terms we use fall into several categories:

- Universals: *always, never, all, everybody*
- Vague action verbs: *know about, understand, appreciate*
- Comparators: *better, newer, cheaper, more*
- Unreferenced pronouns: *they, them, we*

- Unspecified groups: *teachers, parents, things*
- Assumed rules or traditions: *ought, should, must*

When you hear or see such words or phrases in students' speech or writing, ask them to specify, define, or reference their terms. For example,

When you hear . . .	Clarify by probing for specificity:
"He NEVER listens to me."	"Never?" or "Never ever?"
"EVERYBODY has one."	"Everybody?" or "Who, exactly?"
"THINGS go better with . . ."	"Which things, specifically?"
"Things GO better with . . ."	"Go? Go how, specifically?"
"Things go BETTER with . . ."	"Better than what?"
"You SHOULDN'T do that!"	"What would happen if you did?"
"The PARENTS . . ."	"Which parents?"
"I want them to UNDERSTAND."	"What exactly will they be doing if they understand?"
"This cereal is MORE NUTRITIOUS."	"More nutritious than what?"
"THEY won't let me."	"Who is 'they'?"
"The TEACHERS . . ."	"Which teachers?"
"I want him to be NICE."	"Nice? How, specifically, should he be nice?"

Critical thinkers are characterized by their ability to use specific terminology, to refrain from overgeneralizations, and to support their assumptions with valid data. Clarifying and probing by having students use precise language can develop those characteristics (Ennis, 2001).

Gathering Data Through All Senses

By pushing the right biological buttons in the brain, scientists have found they can make the future brighter for many children whose development otherwise would have been stunted. How the buttons work is perhaps the most amazing thing of all. The buttons are the

senses: vision, taste, smell, touch, and sound; and they can be pushed
by experiences from the outside world.

—R. Kotulak

When our senses are dull and sluggish, our thinking is dull and sluggish.
Because all information gets into the head through our sensory pathways,
teachers will want to plan lessons that engage as many of the senses as
possible. For example, "In this lesson, how can I maximize opportunities
to visualize, listen, experience, move, smell, taste, touch, and feel?" The
more senses that are engaged, the greater the learning.

Sensory exercises hone our powers of perception. Consider the following examples:

• Sight. Ninety percent of our sensory input comes through our eyes.
To improve peripheral vision, ask students to shift their eyes from right to
left several times as fast as they can without moving their head. Have them
try to focus on 10 different objects in 10 seconds by scanning the room.
Can they name the objects in the order in which they saw them?

• Touch. Our largest sense organ is our skin. With their eyes closed,
have students feel various textured objects: sandpaper, cotton, silk, steel.
Ask them to describe what they are feeling as they touch it.

• Sound. Although we can't improve our hearing, we can improve
our listening. Have students close their eyes and listen to a single sound.
This exercise will require them to shut out extraneous noise. For example,
as they listen to music, ask them to single out one instrument to follow
(such as the bass guitar or the violin).

• Smell. Provide students with fragrances from various sources: per-
fume, cinnamon, cloves, wintergreen, and eucalyptus. Have them describe what they are smelling. Have them take several small sniffs rather
than sniff deeply. Instruct them to keep their mouths open as they smell.
Drawing the scent into the mouth gives an extra dimension to the smell.

• Taste. Humans taste four basic flavors: sweet, sour, salty, and bitter.
With the students' eyes closed, place a sample of each taste on their
tongue: sugar, lemon juice, salt, and unsweetened chocolate. Have students describe what they taste. Between tastes, cleanse the palate with
crackers, bread, or water.

Creating, Imagining, Innovating

I believe everybody is creative, and everybody is talented. I just don't think that everybody is disciplined. I think that's a rare commodity.

—Al Hirschfield

This extended excerpt from the classroom of Lisa Davis-Miraglia, formerly a teacher in Westorchard Elementary School in Chappaqua, New York, provides a rich example of encouraging ingenuity, originality, and insightfulness:

As my colleagues and I were discussing the literal interpretations many of my students had written about a poem I asked them to reflect on, we began discussing how hard it is to teach someone to think abstractly. Later, as I was thinking back to that conversation, I thought of a comment my friend Raina makes whenever I'm being inflexible. She says, "Lisa, can you please get outside of the box!" That was it! I needed to get my kids to think outside of the box.

The next morning, I put up a slide on the monitor that said, "Think Outside the Box!" Immediately children started to question what I meant. Then I said, "Let me read some examples from last night's homework and you tell me if the person was 'in the box'—which means they were thinking literally—or 'out of the box'—which would mean they were thinking abstractly."

I reread the poem "Alice" by Shel Silverstein and some of the students' written reflections. It was obvious who was "getting" the meaning of literal and abstract and who wasn't. Suddenly, Anna connected it to an activity we did the first week of school.

She said, "This is like the survival kit you gave us on the first day of school. You gave us a rubber band, not so we could band our papers together but to remind us to be flexible in our thinking or to stretch our ideas."

James chimed in, "Oh yeah. Remember, I thought the button was to keep in case a button came off my shirt. And then someone told me that was too obvious, so we switched it to: Remember to button your lips if you have something mean to say or you could use it to button your ideas together—to make connections."

Soon kids were reminding me of other examples from the survival kit. "Yes, yes, yes!" I exclaimed. "Now you're getting it!" My excitement had me jumping in and out of an imaginary box. Then I said, "It's like onions and math!"

Huh? My students looked at me, bewildered. It was if we were all headed in the same direction, and then I decided to switch tracks. Determined—and a firm believer in wait time—I waited. And waited. Finally, Amy said, "They can both make you cry!"

"Yes!" I exclaimed. "How else are onions and math connected?"

Don yelled out, "You can cut the onion into rings and make a Venn diagram out of them."

Laura whispered, "He's in the box."

I offered: "What a great thought, Don, but that is kind of literal because we could actually cut an onion in rings. Keep thinking." Then Beth spoke.

The room got respectfully quiet as we all turned to look at Beth, a special needs child who rarely speaks unless she is absolutely confident that she has a "right" answer. She said, "It's like when you plant onions."

"OK," I encouraged. "Keep going, Beth. Help us see what you're thinking."

"You plant the baby onion in the dirt and it grows," she stated as if the connection was obvious.

"How is that related to math?" I probed for further understanding.

"Well, when you plant the small onion in the ground, it grows. And when you add small numbers together, they grow!"

"Oh, wow, Beth!" I exclaimed. "That is very divergent thinking! Class, is she in the box or out of the box?"

The whole class chimed, "Out of the box!"

The discussion was so powerful that I had to capitalize on the enthusiasm by extending the lesson. When the kids went to the gym, I headed to the kindergarten classroom to borrow the "junk boxes" that they use for sorting. I randomly mixed objects, placing a pile in the middle of each table. When the children returned, I explained that they needed to discuss various attributes of the materials and then sort them—keeping in mind the discussion we had in the morning regarding literal and abstract thinking.

As I circulated, I realized that nearly every table was sorting by the obvious attributes (bikes in one pile, keys in another). I began to ask, "Are you in the box or out of the box?" Some tables rearranged their materials; others stuck with their first ideas.

Whenever I do an activity like this, I do a "three-minute check-in": kids at one table can ask kids at other tables questions to get ideas or to clarify the task. Martin clarified that the task was to sort the objects in a way that wouldn't be obvious to the rest of us. (I have found this strategy to be very beneficial because it takes the onus off me as the only one with the ability to solve problems, and it also requires children to interpret what I've said and explain it in a different way.)

As we circulated from table to table, we had fun trying to figure out how each table sorted its objects. When we got to one table, we were stumped. They had sorted their objects into two piles. One had baseball cards and shells, while the other had keys, buttons, and rocks. Finally, someone yelled out, "Fragile and hard!"

A member of the table confirmed the answer by saying, "We actually named the groups destructible and indestructible with human hands."

As we approached another table where all the items still were mixed together, I impulsively said, "You were supposed to leave your objects in their *sorted* piles!"

Jeremy reminded me to be patient: "We did. They all fit in one category."

Sixteen kids and I stared at the pile of bikes, bugs, keys, cars, and pasta wheels. After many guesses, the table members had to tell us what they were thinking: "The keys are used to start the car, the pasta wheels are in case of a flat, the bugs splat onto the windshield, and the bikes go on the roof when you want to go to the trail to go bike riding. All the items relate to a car!" Now that's getting outside the box!

Students need help in learning how to tap their reservoir of originality and liberate their creative potentials. Techniques such as brainstorming, Mind Mapping®, and metaphorical thinking help to loosen the thinking process. For example, ask a student to describe in what way gravity is like a feather. Or ask how the Escher drawing of people moving up and down the stairs serves as a perfect interpretation for *Romeo and Juliet*. Or ask students to create their own plant and an environment in which it can live. (For further suggestions, refer to such authors as Gordon, 1961; Parnes, 1991; Treffinger & Nassab, 1998; and Treffinger & Nassab, 2000.)

Asking students to find similarities and differences in two or more unlike objects helps them make new connections and find hidden relationships:

- "How does it feel to be a flat tire?"
- "How do you think a zero feels?"
- "Which is crisper: celery or yellow?"
- "Which is the happiest room in your house?

Incorporating such generative questioning as an integral part of any subject matter helps students learn how to initiate creative thought when a situation demands it.

Responding with Wonderment and Awe

> Good teachers are passionate about ideas, learning, and their relationship with students.... These teachers did more than teach to set standards or use approved techniques. Their classroom relationships featured "interest, enthusiasm, inquiry, excitement, discovery, risk taking, and fun." Their cognitive scaffolding of concepts and teaching strategies was "held together with emotional bonds."
>
> —P. Woods and B. Jeffrey, Teachable Moments

Recently a Dutch psychologist tried to figure out what separated chess masters and chess grand masters. He subjected groups of each to a battery of tests: IQ, memory, and spatial reasoning. He found no testing difference between them. In the end, the only difference he found was this: grand masters simply loved chess more. They had more passion and commitment to it. Passion may be the key to creativity (Thornton, 1999).

Enrapture students with awesome phenomena, intriguing situations, and jaw-dropping experiments. Surround them with beautiful scenes, technological marvels, and science fiction. Let their imaginations take flight! What is important about the learning is not so much the content as the enjoyment, enthusiasm, and fascination that students experience about the content. Allow them free range to explore whatever they are intrigued with—as long as they are experiencing the passion.

Invite students to share their interests. What electrifies and mystifies them? In a safe environment, students will feel free to share their fascination, their emotions, and their exhilaration. Make it cool to be passionate about something! Stay with a learning over time, not because the curriculum calls for it but because students have sustained interest in it. Time your lessons so that solutions to problems are not found by the time the bell rings. Instead, allow students to carry their curiosity, ambiguity, and uncertainties over until the next day or class period.

Often students lack the vocabulary to discuss and share their wonderments and fascinations. Their vocabulary for describing such emotions may be limited to such clichés as awesome, cool, amped, and rattled. Teachers can help students extend their range of rich words and descriptive phrases to better express their feelings of wonderment and awe.

Following is a word splash that classifies the vocabulary of "awe" into three levels of intensity. Have your students develop such a list and add more words to each level. Of course, teachers will want to incorporate these words into their own language as they describe experiences in which they were mesmerized.

Mild	Moderate	Strong
Attentive	Fascinated	Stunned
Interested	Curious	Awestruck
Motivated	Amazed	Passionate
	Intrigued	Dazzled
	Excited	Astonished
		Enthralled
		Electrified

This Habit of Mind is probably more caught than taught. Make your lessons lively and animated. Share with your students your fascinations with your content; allow them to see you enthralled and excited about a problem or a discovery and fascinated with your own craft of teaching.

Taking Responsible Risks

Only those who will risk going too far can possibly find out how far one can go.

—*T. S. Eliot*

Students will be more inclined to take risks in an environment that is safe; free from judgment; and accepting of all ideas, human differences, and points of view. Invite students to find examples of risk taking and analyze and report on it. They can look in the fields of athletics (Richard Fosbury), politics (Nelson Mandela), technology (Bill Gates), entertainment (D. W. Griffith), science (Galileo), the arts (Vincent van Gogh), business (J. P. Morgan)—the possibilities are endless.

What was the nature of the risks these people took? Were the risks calculated or spontaneous? What constitutes the differences between calculated and spontaneous risks? Which risks paid off, which did not, and why? Invite students to compare risk taking in various fields: artistic risk taking versus risk taking in space exploration, for example. Which is riskier and why? Which was riskier: Columbus's voyage or Neil Armstrong's? Why?

Read stories and report on adventurers in space, explorers of new lands, social activists, research pioneers, inventors, and artists who were called "cutting edge." Describe their characteristics and the conditions in which they took the risks.

Invite students to describe risks they have taken and the results. When is it appropriate or inappropriate to take a risk? What clues should inform a decision to take risks?

Consider creating a "risk taker's park." Tell students, "We are going to design a new park for risk takers. We will erect five statues dedicated to the greatest risk takers in history in five different fields: social/political, visual/artistic, logical/mathematical, athletic, and literary." Have students work in teams to decide who they want to place in the park and why. Students can also design the park and write letters to the town council or board of supervisors describing why they believe such a park should be built.

Finding Humor

If you can laugh at it, you can live with it.

—Erma Bombeck

Teachers need to build humor into the classroom environment. Create a bulletin board to post funny cartoons, witty sayings, and silly pictures and photos. Let students update the space as they find and contribute new items.

Invite students to be alert to cartoons, comic strips, and jokes that convey one or more of the Habits of Mind. Download from the Web examples of cartoons, videoclips, and humorous commercials. First have students simply enjoy the laughter and humor. Then ask them to analyze what it is that made them laugh.

Share an example of a classroom event in which you (deliberately) generated humor. Describe what went on in your mind to turn it into a hilarious situation.

Develop humor-building rituals. Read comics and cartoons together. Encourage students to cut out, bring to school, and share comics they find especially funny. Agree to watch comedies on television, and ask students to share what made them laugh and what they thought were the most hilarious sequences. Make an album of favorite jokes, cartoons, and sayings. Encourage students to develop their own comic vision and to look for humor in daily life. At the end of the day, ask students to name at least one funny thing they saw or heard that day. Then they can draw a picture that illustrates the funny scene. As you develop lesson plans, ensure that your students will laugh at least three times a day.

Thinking Interdependently

It is good to rub and polish our brain against that of others.

—*Michael De Montaigne*

Working in cooperative groups provides the context for learning many other Habits of Mind. One cannot work with others without the skills of thinking flexibly, listening with understanding and empathy, thinking about thinking (metacognition), thinking and communicating with clarity and precision, and finding humor.

To ensure that students experience positive interdependence, teachers need to structure cooperative learning situations in which children learn the content *and* are responsible for ensuring that all group members succeed in the assigned task. The learning task must be structured to be cooperative and reciprocal. Each member can succeed individually only if all members succeed collectively.

Purposely structure groups heterogeneously to supply a rich mixture of cultures, languages, styles, modalities, points of view, and levels of development. As they resolve their differences, students must engage and practice the Habits of Mind. Set standards for effective group work before the work is assigned, then have students monitor their own and each other's contributions.

After the cooperative task is completed, take time to reflect on how well individuals and groups worked together. What contributed to the group's success? How did each group member contribute to and learn from the experience? Encourage students to give nonjudgmental feedback to each other about their observations. (For further elaboration and suggested activities for learning interdependence, see Johnson & Johnson, 1994; Kagan, 1994; and O'Leary & Dishon, 1998.) A student's poster (see Figure 5.3) summarizes the benefits of thinking interdependently.

FIGURE 5.3
Student Poster

Remaining Open to Continuous Learning

The only thing that we can know is that we know nothing and that is the highest flight of human wisdom.

—*Leo Tolstoy*

There can be no such thing as a mistake; we only learn from experience. In a trusting environment, students reflect on their learnings, analyze their experiences, and apply and transfer learnings to new situations. Probably the most powerful strategy for teaching the habit of remaining open to continuous learning is modeling.

Admit to students that you still are learning about the content, about teaching and learning, about the school as a community, and about them as learners. Share your lesson goals and outcomes with students, and describe your instructional strategies and assessment techniques. Then, at the end of the lesson or unit, invite their feedback about what worked and what didn't.

Demonstrate your own humility through self-modification. Express the learnings you have derived from their feedback about your lesson design and instructional effectiveness. Then, let students see you modify your own behavior based upon your learnings.

You might also ask your students to read about or interview corporate leaders, artists, athletes, and remarkable people who are achieving mastery in their craft (Ames, 1997). What are some indicators that those who have achieved mastery never stop learning? Are they ever complacent about their accomplishments? Or do they reflect George Bernard Shaw's belief that people are wise, not in proportion to their experience but in proportion to their capacity for experience?

References

Ames, J. E. (1997). *Mastery: Interviews with 30 remarkable people*. Portland, OR: Rudra.

Costa, A. (2001). Mediating the metacognitive. In A. Costa (Ed.), *Developing minds: A resource book for teaching thinking* (Rev. ed., pp. 408–412). Alexandria, VA: ASCD.

Costa, A., & Kallick, B. (1995). *Assessment in the learning organization: Shifting the paradigm*. Alexandria, VA: ASCD.

Costa, A., & Marzano, R. (2001). Teaching the language of thinking. In A. Costa (Ed.), *Developing minds: A resource book for teaching thinking* (Rev. ed., pp. 379–383). Alexandria, VA: ASCD.

Ennis, R. (2001). Goals for a critical thinking curriculum. In A. Costa (Ed.), *Developing minds: A resource book for teaching thinking* (pp. 44–46). Alexandria, VA: ASCD.

Gordon, W. (1961). *Synectics: The development of creative capacity*. New York: Grollier.

Johnson, R., & Johnson, D. (1994). *Learning together and alone: Cooperation, competition and individualization*. Needham Heights, MA: Allyn and Bacon.

Kagan, S. (1994). *Cooperative learning*. San Juan Capistrano, CA: Kagan's Cooperative Learning Co.

Laborde, G. (1984). *Influencing with integrity*. Palo Alto, CA: Syntony.

O'Leary, P., & Dishon, D. (1998). *Guidebook for cooperative learning*. Holmes Beach, FL: Learning Publications.

Parnes, S. (1991). Creative problem solving. In A. Costa (Ed.), *Developing minds: Programs for teaching thinking* (Rev. ed., Vol. 2, pp. 54–56). Alexandria, VA: ASCD.

Thornton, J. (1999, January 1–3). Getting inside your head. *Honolulu Advertiser, U.S.A. Weekend Magazine*, pp. 8–9.

Treffinger, D. J., & Nassab, C. A. (1998). *Thinking tool guides*. Sarasota, FL: Center for Creative Learning.

Treffinger, D. J., & Nassab, C. A. (2000). *Thinking tool lessons*. Waco, TX: Prufrock.

6

An Artistic Application
of Habits of Mind

Nadine McDermott

A firm grounding in the arts teaches practical skills and such characteristics as self-discipline and critical thinking. The arts naturally
embrace paradox and ambiguity; to study them is to learn flexible
thinking. Those who have trained in an art form are more likely
not only to grasp the nuances in real life, say the experts, but also
to persevere in finding novel solutions to everyday problems.
—*Susan Gaines, "The Art of Living"*

The schoolroom stage was set at the Bronxville School in Bronxville, New
York: no windows, 52 black chairs, a Steinway grand piano, a portable
chalkboard, students, and teacher. The students arrived to participate in
a music class requiring multidimensional processes that were physical,
intellectual, and emotional. The teacher's goals were clear to her: to teach
these students to sing and to prepare them for a musical performance
twice a year. The students' goals also seemed clear: to enjoy 48 minutes
socializing with their friends and to spend very little time singing.

In typical adolescent fashion, cliques started to surface. More socializing than singing occurred, and the teacher began to feel more like a
referee than an educator. The teacher tried every trick in the educational
bag to create a serious educational learning environment, with limited
success.

This vignette captures the essence of a classroom situation that was very real. Aware that this situation could not continue, I reviewed the curriculum, and, with other department members, I decided to investigate alternative approaches to music education, including assessment. With the *National Standards for Arts Education* (1994) in one hand and the latest research on multiple intelligences (Gardner, 1983) in the other, we knew we had to decide how we could incorporate these essentially new ideas into our work with students. We also decided that we needed to take another look at the traditional method of using biannual performances as "assessment."

Necessary Change

In 1991, department members visited the Pittsburgh Public Schools to observe the Harvard Project Zero Arts PROPEL Pilot Project in action. The educational benefits of this program were obvious and valid. That visit forever changed my perspective of music education and, ultimately, my teaching.

After we returned from Pittsburgh, we agreed as a department to re-create a curriculum that would include alternative forms of assessment contained in a portfolio. After piloting one project from Arts PROPEL, we understood that this new approach required behavioral changes for both the teacher and the students. In monitoring students' growth over time, I discovered that although they were becoming skilled music critics, their behavior didn't change.

Individual and class detentions, telephone calls to parents, and discussions with the administration and my department chair did not remedy the situation. Students continued to act out. Students who came to socialize still held a daily "tea party." Students who truly were interested in learning had difficulty staying interested and retaining skills and concepts because of distractions created by the other students.

What to Do?

The traditional behavioral management plan obviously was not effective. I had to shift my style from punishing students to convincing students to change their behavior in positive directions. The challenge was to find information on this topic so the situation could be remedied.

In the course of my search, a colleague shared with me a handout on the Habits of Mind (at that time called "intelligent behaviors"), which he had received at a workshop. After discussing this handout with members of my department, we made a conscious decision to include the Habits of Mind and Gardner's multiple intelligences as part of the middle and high school music curriculum. The Habits of Mind would be an integral part of the intrapersonal skill development in each music class—skills that would be taught and assessed.

Implementing the Habits of Mind into the traditional 8th grade choral rehearsal was the next hurdle. I was eager to try this new concept, but I struggled with giving up rehearsal time for class discussion on a "nonmusical" topic. What would the benefits be? Would it be possible to change students' behavior this way? I finally summoned enough courage to try.

I began by having the class define the word *habits*. I then passed out a list of the Habits of Mind. We read the habits aloud and considered how behaviors gradually become habits. After a lengthy discussion, which ranged from defining unfamiliar words to how these Habits of Mind could be applied to chorus, I gave students an assignment. I asked them to write a paragraph about each habit, describing how each applied to chorus. As this experiment grew in size and depth, a colleague discovered Theodore Sizer's "intellectual habits" (Sizer, 1992), which we added to our repertoire.

In developing and implementing the nonmusical part of the curriculum, I could see that we were providing tools for students to function more effectively in a large group. I began to think of ways this new concept could be incorporated into rehearsals with purpose and meaning. Ways to assess student progress in this new area soon followed.

I created an assignment that asked the students to describe the similarities and differences between Costa and Kallick's Habits of Mind and Sizer's intellectual habits. In addition, students had to choose two habits and describe how each was illustrated by work in their portfolio. The conclusion of this assignment required students to reflect on their interactions with others in chorus. They had to describe one specific example of a behavior or an attitude that reflected their growth in developing the skills needed for interdependence in an ensemble.

I saw noticeable improvement in students' behavior, which ultimately resulted in improved student performance. Consciously and subconsciously, I modeled the Habits of Mind with and for the students. During rehearsal, I frequently announced when certain Habits of Mind were being modeled. In working with the tenor and bass section in the 8th grade chorus, for example, it was essential that the soprano and alto sections display empathy. The changing adolescent voice is difficult to train. Boys at this age frequently stop singing because they don't know how to use the instrument anymore and because they don't want to be ridiculed by their peers if their voices crack.

Validation

The biannual school concerts proved the benefit of intentionally incorporating the Habits of Mind into rehearsal. The chorus's performance reflected a greater degree of musical precision and accuracy, and the chorus gained respect from the audience and the other ensembles in the department.

The phrase "I don't know" no longer was permitted in class. Students now had strategies to use when an answer was not obvious to them. Students could express uncertainty by saying "I'm not quite sure, but I think the answer might be . . ." or "Could you please restate the question?" I encouraged students to use the Habits of Mind in searching for the solution to a question. This concept provoked students to learn how to learn and thus encouraged independent learning in a large-group setting. The ensemble now functioned more effectively.

As time went on, the Habits of Mind became a strong thread woven into the fabric of every rehearsal. The habits helped increase students' awareness of their behavior so they could monitor themselves, which affected the ensemble positively. We videotaped a portion of a selected piece. While students watched and listened to the videotape, they completed an Arts PROPEL Ensemble Critique from the Arts PROPEL Handbook for Music (Davidson et al., n.d.). This assessment required students to diagnose and prescribe solutions to musical problems. A specific response was essential for a student to score at the advanced level. Coaching students to use all the Habits of Mind during this assessment ultimately improved their performance. My role went from choral "director" to "instructional guide." I created the environment in which independent, self-directed learning occurred in an interdependent, ensemble setting.

Another Opportunity

The true test came when I took a vocal music position in another school district. When students arrived on the first day, I thought I had everything prepared. The students received a handout, clearly outlining the course goals and requirements. After numerous attempts to get their attention, I began doubting what I had learned in my previous position. With a great deal of persistence and flexible thinking, I accomplished the day's plan and admonished those who needed to return with better rehearsal "habits."

This new situation paralleled my previous position in that students were not accustomed to singing in chorus and certainly did not view rehearsal as an academic class. After assessing the class, I identified several weak areas. The students were musically illiterate and vocally untrained. Their perceptions about chorus were casual at best. All the evidence pointed toward a need for exposure to the Habits of Mind.

Weighing all the factors, I decided to introduce the Habits of Mind to the accelerated chorus first. These students had auditioned the previous year and were selected to be members of this ensemble. These 23 students were in the class because of their commitment and willingness to accept the challenge of taking a high school course in middle school. I quickly discovered that was not the case entirely! They, too, were not taking chorus to become skilled, trained musicians.

To introduce the Habits of Mind, I followed the same lesson plan that I had used in my previous district, but I added a reflective journal component. I left time at the end of rehearsal for students to reflect on what Habits of Mind they had used and how they had used them. We shared the reflections at the beginning of the next rehearsal. Rehearsals became more productive, and all but a few students began to realize the positive changes.

To ensure that these Habits of Mind remained an integral part of every rehearsal, I developed a daily plan, a type of itinerary that delineated our musical objectives and asked a guiding question about what Habits of Mind would be used to reach our musical destination. I first shared this approach with students using a song for which we had very little time to prepare for the performance. The students had to maintain a daily journal. In the sample student journal entries presented here, I have added in brackets the Habits of Mind the students were describing. Here are the entries:

> I think that I have a better understanding of what we have to accomplish and in what amount of time. I hope this is another interesting way to learn music that I can carry with me to learn other pieces of music [applying past knowledge]. I think by limiting us to four days, we all focused on doing things right the first time [accuracy and precision].

> I feel that if the Select Choir continues to behave like this during class, our spring concert will be extremely rewarding. I also learned that I can retain music faster. I feel that the journal entries force us to reevaluate what we did in class and focus on the areas that we need help with [metacognition]. By doing this and becoming aware of our mistakes, we are forcing ourselves to pay particularly close attention to these areas and correcting our mistakes [accuracy and precision, metacognition, persistence]. It only took me 5 periods, 210 minutes, less than 4 hours to learn this piece of music. I am excited with my progress as a musician.

These student examples reflect the initial stage of this new way of thinking and behaving. The impact was obvious, and I was compelled by students' rapid progress. For these reasons, I incorporated the Habits of Mind into every lesson and into every assessment. As a result, a common language developed among the ensemble members. They also developed a mutual understanding of how musicians were to behave in rehearsal. One student wrote, "I believe that some of the simplest skills that I learned in that room will guide me through some of the most difficult parts of my life in the future." Another student wrote, "I don't know is not an acceptable answer. In class, you must try to answer the question by drawing on past knowledge." Another wrote, "I am glad we learned these [Habits of Mind] because I became more conscientious about the way that I acted in school. I learned how to become a better student." This validation was incentive enough for me to refine the implementation of the Habits of Mind in rehearsal.

The Second Year

Knowing that I was getting a new group of students who were not familiar with the Habits of Mind, I realized I had to introduce the habits within the first month. In doing so, I saw a very responsive group of students ready to meet the challenges that were ahead. One student proclaimed, "Habits of Mind are used every day to help me reach my goals. In order to overcome my weaknesses, metacognition is very important. Using Habits of Mind doesn't necessarily mean you know all of the answers, but it means you know what to do when you don't know the answer." Another student remarked, "The Habits of Mind helped me a great deal to organize my thinking. I have used flexibility in thinking to help me realize that there is not always one way of doing something. It has taught me to think about the different solutions to a problem before rushing ahead with the first solution I come up with."

The level of productivity in rehearsal increased tremendously. Students more consistently demonstrated the behaviors of musicians. When I used the phrase "demonstrate the Habits of Mind of a musician" in rehearsal, the response was immediate: students sat with correct posture, and they held their music correctly, pencil in hand, prepared for their first entrance.

Musicians' Habits of Mind

Training students to become skilled musicians is a complex task, both cognitive and physical in nature. Decoding the music symbol system requires the same process of sound-symbol correspondence as reading. (For example, in reading, "This is what the word looks like, and this is what it sounds like." In music, "This is what the musical phrase looks like, and this is what it sounds like.") A musician literally must "think in sound." While the cognitive processes of thinking in sound are taking place, the musician is also producing the sound either by playing an instrument, which is an extension of the body, or by using the voice, which is an intangible instrument. A musician must condition the mind, which conditions the body to physically produce the sound, while at the same time cognitively decoding the notation in the musical score to create musical meaning. These complex functions of mind and body require the musician to use metacognition to experience growth and progress.

The Habits of Mind create an avenue for students to organize their thinking as musicians. Throughout students' training, I intentionally identify the attributes of musicians from both a cognitive and a physical aspect. The following journal entries reflect how students used the habits to organize their thinking:

> During the winter concert, we learned how to assign solfège syllables to the notes. In preparation for the spring concert, we drew on past knowledge and assigned solfège syllables to the notes in our new songs.

> Curiosity led us down another path of exploration. If there was an unfamiliar symbol somewhere in the music, we identified the symbol and its purpose.

> I believe one of the Habits of Mind that has helped us the most was decreasing impulsivity. Since the beginning of the year, we have all become so much more independent, yet we can still work well together as an ensemble. Before, if we had a question, our hands would shoot up and a lot of teacher calling and "ooohhhhing" would go on. Now, when we have a question, we think about it and listen to others. Only if it is extremely important and pertains to the lesson do we finally ask the question. We no longer have to waste time on inappropriate questions and pointless babble.

> Almost each and every day, our choir used persistence while learning this piece. It takes a great deal of effort to continuously work

hard and not get frustrated. Our choir, though we did not sing everything correctly at first glance, persevered until we got it right.

I have used flexibility in thinking to help me realize that there is not always one way of doing something. It has taught me to think about the different solutions to a problem before rushing ahead with the first solution I come up with.

Checking for accuracy and precision was another intelligent behavior used in learning this piece. The choir continued to work and strive for the goal to make "America the Beautiful" as accurate and precise as we could, and we would not settle for anything less.

When Habits of Mind are embedded in the learning process of becoming a musician, the end product for students is empowerment to learn. Metacognition allows students to self-reflect, assess, and direct their own learning. Their experience is rich with strategies and multiple solutions. The study of music promotes inductive as well as deductive reasoning because many musical problems have more than one correct solution.

The *National Standards for Arts Education* clearly outline what students should know and be able to do. The skills, concepts, and knowledge to meet those standards cannot be obtained in a traditional rehearsal setting. Only through the Habits of Mind (and alternative forms of assessment) are my students able to meet those standards and, even more, become highly skilled, intelligent musicians.

References

Davidson, L., Myford, C., Plasket, D., Scripp, L., Swinton, S., Torff, B., & Waanders, J. (n.d.). *Arts PROPEL handbook for music.* Pittsburgh, PA: Pittsburgh Public School System.

Gardner, H. (1983). *Frames of mind.* New York: BasicBooks.

National standards for arts education: What every young American should know and be able to do in the arts. (1994). Reston, VA: Music Educators National Conference.

Sizer, T. (1992). *Horace's school: Redesigning the American high school.* New York: Houghton Mifflin.

7

Habits of Mind
as Character Education

Curtis Schnorr

In recent years, schools have been challenged to teach character education, which encompasses moral values and good citizenship. This charge sent many districts searching for programs to implement their state and local mandates. Though they found a variety of options to meet their needs, I believe their search should have started—and ended—with the Habits of Mind.

Some may ask: Why should thinking be the foundation for a character education program? I have a better question: Why *shouldn't* thinking be the foundation? Successful character education is grounded in thoughtful processes. Schools need to develop climates that support and foster these thinking processes, just as they support development of students who are productive citizens with strong character. The Habits of Mind can help achieve all these goals.

The Need for Character Development

In *Educating for Character*, Thomas Likona (1991) observes, "Until recently, calls for school reform have focused on academic achievement. Now we know that character development is needed as well" (p. 22). Likona bases his arguments on troubling trends among youth. He also bases his arguments on the belief that if schools want to do one thing to improve teachers' lives, they will make moral education—

including the creation of a civil, humane school community—the center of school life.

A brochure from the Maryland State Department of Education (1998) supports this idea: "Character education is not a program—it's a way of life. Character education will come in a variety of forms. The ideal approach should be to infuse character education into the daily operation of the school" (p. 1). Elias and colleagues (1997) concur with this idea: "Social and emotional competence is the ability to understand, manage, and express the social/emotional aspects of one's life in ways that enable the successful management of life tasks such as learning, forming relationships, solving everyday problems, and adapting to complex demands of growth and development" (p. 2).

Let there be no confusion: development of a classroom and school environment that is safe and orderly for both students and teachers is at the root of character education. As Alfie Kohn (1996) observes, "How students act in class is so intertwined with curricular content that it may be a folly even to talk about classroom management or discipline as a field unto itself" (p. 21). Kohn further asks, "How can we deny that the way children act in a classroom is significantly related to their interest in what they've been given to do? Tapping and extending that interest takes time and talent, patience and skill and even courage" (p. 21). Curwin and Mendler (1988) summarize this concept well: "Every decision affecting behavior management also affects instruction" (p. 20).

We want students to use what they learn to solve all kinds of problems—new *and* old. Many school administrators agree that the majority of office visits occur because students fail to solve problems in a thoughtful manner. This concern leads to another important question: How do human beings "behave intelligently," and how does this affect character education and behavior management? I believe our work at Friendship Valley Elementary School in Westminster, Maryland, answers both these questions.

Character Education at Friendship Valley

Between 1994 and 2000, Friendship Valley's enrollment increased almost 30 percent, yet office referrals for discipline did not rise proportionally.

In fact, behavior referrals still declined when student enrollment went to a school high of more than 750 students. We believe the most important factor contributing to this decline was development of a thoughtful student body that (1) used intelligent behaviors and (2) took time to think before taking action.

Students have learned to stop and think before they act because teachers and administrators at Friendship Valley constantly ask these questions:

• What intelligent behavior did you *not* use that resulted in a classroom or school problem?

• What intelligent behavior could you use to prevent future incidents?

Students with office referrals are asked to complete a problem-solving sheet that includes those same two questions. Depending on their grade level, students have to respond either in writing or orally to a school administrator concerning their use (or lack of use) of the Habits of Mind. Following are some of our reflections on the Habits of Mind gained through these interactions with students.

Persisting. (Stick to it.) Students who are persistent do not give up easily. They stick to an activity until the end. Students exhibiting persistence are less likely to stray off task, and they are less likely to interrupt the learning environment for others. As students increase their persistence, they focus more on thinking, and they are less likely to cause classroom and school disruptions.

Managing impulsivity. (Take your time.) Teachers encourage students to use "think time" before offering an answer. Students need to practice using think time to decrease their impulsivity in everything they do. Consider how many times impulsive students interrupt the learning environment. How many office referrals are the result of students' impulsivity? As students reduce their impulsivity, they are less likely to enter into arguments with others, and they are more likely to focus on the task at hand.

Listening with understanding and empathy. (Understand others.) When we take time to listen to others, we take time to understand them. When we understand others, we are less likely to get into disagreements. We need to teach students how to listen to others. Listening provides the opportunity to empathize with others and to understand their point of view.

Thinking flexibly. (Look at it another way.) Students often have difficulty envisioning alternatives. Without alternative points of view, they become rigid in their thinking. Rigid thinking prevents students from generating open-minded responses to various social situations. Teachers and administrators need to provide students opportunities for practicing and demonstrating flexible thinking, which fosters a tolerance of others.

Thinking about thinking (metacognition). (Know your knowing.) When students become aware of their own thinking, they begin to understand that their way may not always be the best or only way. Students who take time to understand their own thinking develop an appreciation for and understanding of the thinking and actions of others.

Striving for accuracy. (Look over your work.) Students who take the time to check for accuracy are less likely to act impulsively. They check their facts and the sources of information before taking action. Checking for accuracy deters students from responding to rumors and false accusations. Checking for accuracy also provides students necessary think time.

Questioning and posing problems. (Work it out.) Taking the time to question and problem solve prevents student disputes and disagreements. Students who problem solve become more thoughtful, respectful citizens. Problem solvers are less impulsive in their actions and responses to others.

Applying past knowledge to new situations. (Use what you learn.) By using prior knowledge, students are less prone to repeat poor choices or mistakes. Students using prior knowledge learn from their past experiences. They exhibit a greater sense of thoughtfulness as they encounter problems and difficulties with others.

Thinking and communicating with clarity and precision. (Be clear.) Students who develop a precision of language and thought clearly communicate their ideas, intentions, and actions to others. Clear communication eliminates many misunderstandings. Precision of language also can prevent many disputes that occur in the classroom, on the playground, and in the cafeteria.

Gathering data through all senses. (Use natural pathways.) Students who use all their senses take the time to examine issues from all viewpoints. They listen to problems, but they also seek out confirming information visually before taking positive action.

Creating, imagining, innovating. (See things differently.) Creative students solve differences in a more thoughtful manner. They seek alternate solutions to classroom and school issues. Creative problem solvers seek alternate solutions to problems they encounter during the school day. They resort less to classroom and playground disruptions.

Responding with wonderment and awe. (Have fun working it out.) By enjoying problem solving, students do not let themselves get burdened by life's little problems. They see problems as opportunities to enhance their thinking skills.

Taking responsible risks. (Seek adventure with responsibility.) Students often take irresponsible risks on the playground and in the classroom. This tendency endangers the safety, well-being, and personal space of others around them. Responsible risk takers plan and think carefully before taking risks in any situation.

Finding humor. (Pursue joy and laughter.) Students who know the value of humor do not let themselves get overburdened with the minor traumas and vicissitudes of everyday life. Instead, they seek pleasure in the world around them. They learn to use humor intelligently to diffuse classroom and playground problems.

Thinking interdependently. (Work together.) When students work, plan, and think together, they expand their thinking and develop a strong learning environment. By working together, students develop an appreciation for the talents and skills of those around them. They begin to value their classmates' contributions.

Remaining open to continuous learning. (Keep your mind growing.) Teachers need to model the importance of lifelong learning. Students need to see teachers fascinated by the joy and wonderment of new learning. As they develop this habit, students will remain open to the contributions, thoughts, and teaching from those around them.

Costa (1991) observes that the search for intelligent life will lead to students who "display cognizant and compassionate behavior toward other life forms as they are able to understand the need for protecting their environment, respecting the roles and values of other human beings, and perceiving the delicate worth, uniqueness, and relationships of everything and everyone they encounter" (p. 30). The goal of character education should be the creation of compassionate, thoughtful, humane students. Above all, thoughtful students are the key to fostering learning environments that place a premium on thinking, which results in intelligent student behavior.

References

Costa, A. (1991). *The school as a home for the mind.* Palatine, IL: Skylight.

Curwin, R., & Mendler, A. (1988). *Discipline with dignity.* Alexandria, VA: ASCD.

Elias, M., Zins, J., Weissberg, R., Frey, K., Greenberg, M., Haynes, N., Kessler, R., Schwab-Stone, M., & Shriver, T. (1997). *Promoting social and emotional learning: Guidelines for educators.* Alexandria, VA: ASCD.

Kohn, A. (1996). *Beyond discipline: From compliance to community.* Alexandria, VA: ASCD.

Likona, T. (1991). *Educating for character.* New York: Bantam.

Maryland State Department of Education. (1998). *Character education* [brochure]. Baltimore, MD: Author.

8

Using Habits of Mind to Look "Inside the Text"

Kathleen C. Reilly

Secondary school English departments often strain at the seams from the weight of covering so much material. They are called upon to strengthen grammar basics, promote the importance of spelling, reinforce punctuation rules, and guide students in the purposeful study of literature. These many responsibilities weighed on my mind when I decided to integrate the Habits of Mind with the study of literature and writing in my 12th grade classroom. All the signs indicated that bad things could happen to a good idea if I allowed it to get lost among all the other demands on my time.

Even though my teaching days already were overloaded, I was drawn to research about critical-thinking methods. Adolescence is mysterious, for sure, and I had decided that although all my students *could* experience high-level thinking, they simply were not disposed to do it. When I began to introduce thinking skills, students tenaciously expressed the belief that thinking critically was a "natural" gift. In many cases, even those who saw themselves as "good students" felt the process was beyond their skills. I was driven by the question of why my students resisted problem solving and decision making.

The First Year

When I first introduced thinking skills to my students, I announced that we were going to use a metaphor as a way to "look inside" the texts we were studying. We started with an exercise on metaphors that we live by, then easily moved into a search for metaphors in the texts we studied. Most interesting, I think, were student responses to my questions about specific metaphors to describe our classroom. They immediately mentioned the placement of my desk in the back of the room, and they told me confidently that ours was a "student-centered classroom." They extended this metaphor when they noted my selection of seminar tables instead of desks to encourage collaboration. They also noted the way I sat in different places among them, not in front of them.

Many other classroom elements served as metaphors for my students. For example, they saw the quotations hanging on the walls as metaphors for my expectations. They were particularly drawn to a passage by Annie Dillard: "Why are we reading—if not in hopes of beauty laid bare and life's darkest mysteries probed?" They also pointed to Hannah Arendt's words: "Welcome to a place of excellence . . . where we come together to be the best we can be." Other elements suggested some serious work that would remain after they left the classroom: individual portfolios, dialectic notebooks along the window shelves, and favorite childhood drawings that prompted an early writing assignment.

Refining My Teaching

When that year of metaphor ended, I wanted to get involved further with ways to teach critical thinking. This curiosity led to another academic year of refining my teaching for thinking and discovering ways that students could learn and apply methods. Building on my work with Bena Kallick, I set out to design specific instructional strategies aimed at developing various habits of mind. I read a variety of research in the areas of cognition and metacognition. I knew from experience that effective thinking has certain identifiable characteristics, and I was convinced that thoughtful classroom instruction could create the climate to teach those characteristics.

Teaching for thinking simply means that teachers strive to develop classroom conditions conducive to student thinking. Teachers pose problems and raise questions, and then follow up by introducing dilemmas, paradoxes, and discrepancies for students to resolve. Teachers also structure the classroom environment for thinking: they value thinking, make time for it, support it, and assess student growth in it. Teaching for thinking assumes a classroom atmosphere that balances trust, risk taking, and originality. I am confident this environment can be created anywhere because it is established through the behavior of a teacher who models respect for intelligence and establishes the clear, convincing expectation that all students can become better thinkers. In this kind of classroom you find an almost palpable sense of community that stems from collaboration and open investigation of ideas.

I planned to construct exercises that would provide a frame for analysis of literature, writing, self-evaluation, and observation. This construct was based on the knowledge that it is possible to connect teachable skills to a student's potential for responding to problems and ambiguities. I wanted to guide my students to recognize intelligent behavior, both academic and personal, as they approached the formation of argument for the expository essay. I also wanted them to recognize instances where literary characters reacted to conflict and resolved difficulties intelligently. I believed that if students could identify and articulate the ways in which characters used, or needed to use, more intelligent behavior, the students would begin to deepen their own understandings of the literary devices of character motivation, the author's choice of conflict, and thematic implications.

As we searched texts for clues about the connection between habits of mind and narrative development, I asked my students how they thought about their own work. What habits did they identify as essential to quality work? This was organic, really; it flowed naturally out of the literary analysis. Students came up with these habits: reading carefully, using dialectic notebooks to record intuitive responses, anticipating questions to clarify during class discussion, taking notes to record interpretation, and recognizing similarities to other works they'd read.

Gatsby and the Habits of Mind

When good thinkers study a text, they feel a sense of investigation, a deep curiosity, and an insistence on being accurate. Yet my one question remained: although most of my students seemed to have the same ability to probe and discover the text, why didn't they do so? While we were studying *The Great Gatsby*, I asked students in my Advanced Senior Writing Seminar to analyze the novel in terms of Costa and Kallick's Habits of Mind. Beginning with basic discussions of the kinds of behavior apparent in the novel's main characters, they seemed to recognize quickly Jay Gatsby's creativity and persistence, Nick Carraway's wonderment and ability to listen to others, and Daisy Buchanan's impulsivity.

Moving beyond surface evaluations, I asked them to consider how the characters could have behaved more intelligently and to name alternative strategies the characters could have used. With their texts in one hand and the list of the Habits of Mind in the other, they explored the novel with little help from me. All their observations were formed first by their close reading of the text. But their understanding deepened when they pointed to specific instances where a systematic method of problem solving would have changed the direction of the novel's tragic outcome.

For example, they acknowledged that Nick Carraway had the advantages of being a careful listener and of drawing on past knowledge to change the course of his own life. This observation prompted them to think about themselves and their choices. In the course of this exploration, I saw a shift in the classroom from the teacher asking all the questions to students asking questions about the characters, which propelled further discussion. How did Nick make up his mind about Gatsby? What questions did Nick ask? How creative was Gatsby beyond his conception of himself?

Eventually, students drifted into conversations about their own Habits of Mind. Typically I would ask, "How, in fact, did you make up your mind about Nick? In what specific ways did you think about this novel? What were the literary devices that helped you to uncover character motivation and, going further, to think about your own behavior, your own choices?"

In developing their essays about Nick, students were drawn to his steady voice in the midst of chaos. They decided his strength was his ability to approach conflict in alternate ways. Nick maintains his loyalty to Gatsby, even when all others have abandoned Gatsby, and he is mature in the face of the disorder around him. Nick is not a gossip or a judge as he perseveres in his commitment to ensure that Gatsby's funeral be appropriate to his "romantic readiness." Students responded instinctively to Nick's allegiance to Gatsby when others just used his friend. Many of the students shared personal stories about times when they were compelled to stick by a friend when their own definition of loyalty was tested.

Sitting alone in my classroom at the end of June, I realized that I had waited too long to begin applying the Habits of Mind in our work. I was unsure about the short story as an entry point to the habits, and I lost about 10 weeks of what could have been very productive time. Obviously, the time was not totally wasted. I was helping students get accustomed to the vocabulary, breaking down the Habits of Mind, and working with selected habits. I know that the trust was there, and the playfulness of exercises like this appealed to students, especially because adolescent interest in learning more about the self is at its peak in 12th grade.

Though I regretted the lost time, I greatly valued the work we did. The essays analyzing *The Great Gatsby* were richer and more original because students had the power to criticize and suggest. The Habits of Mind became the touchstones for character analysis, and students gained a sense of power as they made resonant connections to their own behaviors. Students became enraged at Gatsby's naïvely romantic pursuit of Daisy, but they also defined what they knew about his flaws by using the habits as a frame. When they hypothesized about ideas, they arrived at much more pleasing and mature essays: "If Gatsby had been less impulsive, funneled his creativity into more than romance, recognized the strength of his creativity, then . . . ."

In the future, I'll begin work immediately in the fall by introducing the Habits of Mind and working them into all of our writing assignments, from the argumentative essay to the analysis of all literary genres. This time I will not hold back, because I know that I can rely on my curiosity and wonder to help students rediscover their own. Literature is the perfect conduit to understanding the self, a lesson I learn again and again with my students' help!

9

Foreign Language Instruction and the "Sense-Sational" Habits of Mind

Gina Celeste Costa

Consider the following three stories, which originally were presented to students in a foreign language class learning Spanish:

> Juan's class wants to have a party. Juan offers to go to the store. He drives his Ferrari to the local Safeway. He is in a great hurry. Juan grabs some chips and soda and throws them into the cart. Then he rushes to the deli section and tosses some mild red chili salsa into the cart. He runs to the checkout counter and pays $20 for the snacks and drives back to school. The students look at the food and say, "Yum!" Juan opens the mild red chili salsa. The students dip in their chips and put them in their mouths. "AYYYYY!!!" they shout. The salsa is mislabeled! It is really EXTRA, EXTRA HOT! The teacher calls the fire department! The firefighters spray water all over the students. The principal gets mad at the teacher and the class goes home.

> Katerina is very, very tired. She decides to go to bed. She brushes her teeth, washes her face, and puts on her pajamas. She checks the doors, picks up the cat, and turns off all the lights. She hops into bed, caresses the cat, and closes her eyes for the night. Suddenly, she sits bolt upright in her bed! There is a very loud sound

coming from the house next door! She realizes that it is the sound of snoring! She jumps out of bed, throws open the window, and shouts at the man to stop snoring! The man stops for a while. Soon the sound of snoring is too loud for Katerina to bear! She calls the police, and they arrest Katerina's neighbor and haul him off to jail. Finally Katerina goes to sleep peacefully and doesn't wake up until noon the next day.

Valerie is in Paris. She will be there for three days and nights. She is so excited because it is her first trip to the City of Lights. She plans to visit many places, but what she really wants to do is see the lights of the city from the top of the Eiffel Tower. The first night Valerie tries to get a taxi to the tower, but none is available. The second night she takes the subway to the tower, but the elevator workers there are on strike and she cannot go up. The third night Valerie is very worried. She really wants to see the city all lit up! Once again she arrives at the tower. The line is terribly long! She feels someone tapping on her shoulder. She whirls around and sees a man in a bright red cape! It's Superman! He points to her and points to the top of the tower. Suddenly, Valerie feels herself flying through the cool air. She lands on top of the tower! She looks down and sees the lights of Paris glittering below her. Valerie is very, very happy.

What's going on with these "sense-sational" stories? They're just the usual fare in a foreign language classroom that employs all the senses, engages the mind, activates humor, and involves students physically and emotionally as they learn vocabulary and grammar structures in an exciting context. This new approach to foreign language acquisition draws on many of the Habits of Mind, and it is nothing like the traditional way many of us studied foreign languages when we were in high school.

The Grammatical Approach

Many of us remember when foreign languages were taught using a purely grammatical approach. Students received vocabulary lists to memorize, and sometimes the lists were reinforced with pictures or examples of the words. Grammar structures and verb tenses were taught by presentations, explanations, note taking, worksheets, and drill. All of these benefited few, and only a small percentage of students mastered them.

None of these methods involved the whole student. The language didn't come alive, and students didn't engage their senses, emotions, or bodies. Yet foreign language teachers continued to teach this way. They reasoned that they had learned successfully in this manner, and their students should succeed, too. Over the years, the number of students who continued with language classes decreased, until only a tiny fraction remained in the higher levels. Schools in effect limited their foreign language programs to students with the most well-developed study skills, and many assumed that others couldn't—and wouldn't—be successful.

A New Approach

Fortunately, using all the senses has become more common in foreign language teaching, and this approach has enabled students with a variety of abilities to succeed. Essentially, we all acquired our first language through using all our senses. Studies show that even before a child is born, the child feels and recognizes the rhythm of language. After birth, the baby continues to see, hear, and feel language without, of course, being expected to produce it until the baby is ready.

When a child utters that first word, parents are ecstatic—even if the word is pronounced incorrectly. Few parents would even consider correcting a baby saying "dada" instead of "daddy." Yet as the child grows older, much language acquisition is through response to commands.

"Come here and give Grandma a kiss!" exclaims Grandma as she points to her cheek. Soon the baby notices that a kiss leads to a hug and squeals of delight from Grandma.

"Don't pull the kitty's tail! Pet her nicely, like this," says Mom as she takes the baby's hand and shows the proper way to pet a cat. Soon the child learns that the soft, fluffy thing that sleeps on the couch all day is called a kitty.

"Stay away from the stove! It's hot, hot, hot!" Dad warns as he cooks spaghetti. The baby soon associates the steam coming from the pot with Dad's warning of danger and that "hot" can hurt.

At this stage, the child is receptive to language in all its forms: spoken and unspoken, through expressions, emotions, and body movements. The child receives "comprehensible input," which is stored for the day when the child is ready to use the language to communicate verbally (Krashen & Terrell, 1983).

An Active, Creative Start

In my foreign language classroom at Dixon High School in Dixon, California, I use commands that require listening and responding with understanding. I find that they are a useful starting point in teaching vocabulary and advancing the acquisition of a second language. Beginning students are asked to respond to commands, but they are not asked to produce spoken language (Ray & Seely, 1997).

I try to make this stage as active, vivid, humorous, and creative as possible. I say much more than just "touch your nose, touch your toes, stand up, sit down, look to the left, look to the right." The commands should be as lively as the teacher can make them (Ray & Seely, 1997). Consider these examples:

- "Put your belly button on the ceiling and wave at it!"
- "Point to the teacher and laugh."
- "Go to McDonald's and buy a hamburger. Smell the hamburger, and take a big bite. Yum!"
- "Kiss the floor."
- "Throw the ball at the door."
- "Put the teacher in the trash can."

Students receive comprehensible input, react to the commands, and store vocabulary in their long-term memory because they are reacting to it physically. They're having a great time in class, too. At this point, no written production is expected—a point you may have to explain to parents.

Eventually, students need and are ready to hear, see, and acquire vocabulary in a specific context. Now they are ready to work with short stories, like the ones at the beginning of this chapter. These stories make the second language come alive (Ray & Seely, 1997), and they are designed to engage the senses. For example, the story of the hot salsa engages the sense of taste. Katerina's snoring story engages listening. Valerie's Paris adventure engages visual, tactile, and kinesthetic senses.

Before asking students to create such a story, the teacher presents main words or phrases to be included. Each of these "language chunks" is assigned a physical motion that, after repeated practice, the student will associate with the new vocabulary (Ray & Seely, 1997). A hand up to the ear can indicate hearing, fingers pinching the nose can symbolize stinking, and an arm thrust forward can mean throwing. Students also benefit when you give them something in their first language to connect with the new word. For example, if you're teaching the Spanish word for "to think," *pensar*, children can draw forth past knowledge to relate it to "pensive" or "penny for your thoughts." After students practice the movements, the teacher presents the story and students act it out, using the physical motions (Ray & Seely, 1997).

In the story about Juan and the mislabeled salsa, the students empathize with Juan. They intentionally use the motions and the new vocabulary to buy, open, smell, taste, react in horror to, and be rescued from the extra hot salsa that Juan brings from the store. Of course, there is no actual salsa, but the students pretend to hold the salsa in their hands as they visualize and "taste" it. They also internalize the new vocabulary associated with the salsa in the story.

When acting out the situation about Katerina and the snorer, the class snores loudly and rudely with great delight. Students use the sense of hearing, and they are annoyed by the excessive snoring. The police tear into the classroom and yank the snorer away. Katerina finally gets some sleep, and all the while the students employ reflexive verbs without even realizing it.

In the third story, students playing the lucky Valerie finally fly through the air feeling the cool Paris air on their faces. They see the glittering lights in the world's most romantic city. The next step is for students to tell the story to each other in pairs, using the main words and phrases as a guide (Ray & Seely, 1997). It's a lot of fun watching students try to draw forth a word or an expression using motion to aid their memory.

Several other steps are designed to motivate students' thinking in the target language and to improve their spoken proficiency. One of these involves questioning techniques designed to elicit the students' use of the vocabulary and to check their comprehension of the facts presented in the story. Students call out answers to questions. The questions can be in true/false form, such as "The salsa is blue, right?" to which they will say, "No! It's red!" Or the students may be challenged to choose among several possibilities: "Is the salsa blue, white, or red?" Of course, they will shout, "Red!" Finally, the questions may be designed to have the students produce facts. For example, I simply may ask, "The color of the salsa is . . . ?" Once again, the answer is "Red!" (Ray & Seely, 1997).

The language in the stories can be serious or ludicrous, as long as it provides students with usable vocabulary. At this point, the whole world, figuratively speaking, can be brought into the classroom. Students will best remember and enjoy any words or phrases that engage the senses:

- A cuddly kitten biting your finger with its teeny, tiny teeth
- The acrid smell of cigarettes on a crowded European train
- The mouthwatering aroma of barbecuing steaks coming from the house next door
- An air conditioner that breaks when the temperature is 100 degrees
- The Spanish teacher listening to the Beatles when the students prefer the Spice Girls

Absolutely any vocabulary can be acquired in the foreign language classroom through visualizing, imagining, using appropriate props, and using a physical action to effect long-term retention. The best part, of course, is students' enthusiasm and their realization that they really are learning. They are excited and proud when they can draw from their memory a word or an expression several months after a lesson, with the help of the motions.

All teachers, regardless of subject area, can enhance their students' learning by using this Habit of Mind: gathering data through all senses. It is my hope that through the sensory processes of role playing, moving, touching, smelling, tasting, and envisioning, students can enhance their self-knowledge, become aware of how they learn best, and apply that knowledge in their continuous, lifelong learning.

References

Krashen, S. D., & Terrell, T. D. (1983). *The natural approach: Language acquisition in the classroom*. Hayward, CA: Alemany Press.

Ray, B., & Seely, C. (1997). *Fluency through TPR storytelling*. Berkeley, CA: Command Performance Language Institute.

10

Discovering Habits of Mind in Mathematics

Carol T. Lloyd

Perhaps this story is familiar to you. I teach in North Carolina, where the state mandates curriculum for every subject and every grade, which teachers are required by law to follow. The state also mandates an end-of-grade testing program for grades 3 through 8 and end-of-course testing for grades 9 through 12. These tests, of course, are based on the prescribed curriculum. School systems, individual schools, and, to some extent, even individual teachers are evaluated on students' scores on these tests. Obviously, this structure leaves little freedom for individual schools or teachers to spend much time outside the mandated curriculum.

The good news, however, is that this lack of freedom is pushing needed curriculum changes. The state implements new math curricula every five years, which also has changed the corresponding testing program. These changes include testing students on their abilities to use the calculator as a tool for solving problems, to communicate mathematical ideas with words and drawings, and to solve various types of problem situations. To gain time for teaching such operations and processes, we have deemphasized mastery of basic skills that can be done by calculators. It's more important for students to be able to take a problem situation, organize it for input into the calculator, and use the resulting answers or graphs for data analysis and prediction. As we move toward more of this kind of mathematical thinking, it's obvious that classrooms must nourish the development of the Habits of Mind.

Supporting the Habits of Mind

Since 1991, I have worked on developing the Habits of Mind with my students. I know I must support students by pointing out examples of where the Habits of Mind have been used, showing where they could have been used, and providing opportunities for students to display the habits. I also know that I constantly must model these behaviors. Students should see their teacher experience failure. They should see their teacher model persistence, metacognition, a sense of humor, and then flexibility by applying a number of problem-solving strategies until finding one that works. Through these performances, students see how I achieve a greater level of problem-solving efficacy, and they see how they can attain the same kind of successes.

Students who do not feel efficacious about their ability to succeed often are unwilling to tackle problem situations. Yet students must accept responsibility for their own learning. They need opportunities to figure things out on their own or with the help of other students. I must not jump in too quickly to answer their questions or solve their problems. Assignments should be completed for the contribution they make to the student's learning process, not just to satisfy me.

I have observed students' sense of efficacy grow as they experience success in an environment that scaffolds their learning, encourages "failing forward," and keeps the risk taker safe from humiliation. One student, Mia, came to me as a sophomore quite sure that math was not her subject. She was an excellent student in all classes, but she felt math was her weakness. She saw it as something to be tolerated because she had no choice. Her attitude changed a great deal because of her experiences in my class. In fact, by the time she reached advanced math her junior year, she had become the one the other students turned to for help—and she knew she could help them.

Students become interdependent by working in an environment that requires them to be interdependent and rewards them for being so. The classroom environment should support the idea of "a journey we are taking together," not "teacher versus students" or "student versus student." The teacher should not be viewed as the person with all the answers. Groups of students (and their teachers) should be viewed as a learning community. Once again, the teacher's modeling is extremely important. The teacher must model the idea that we are all smarter together than we are alone. Students should see teachers working together with other teachers and with students to plan and solve all types of activities and problems. Students should also be asked for their input. For example, students can easily provide the teacher with feedback about classroom procedures and activities. Cooperative learning techniques also give students practice with interdependent behaviors they will be required to use outside the classroom.

Activities that develop students' problem-solving abilities support the Habits of Mind of metacognition, flexibility, and precision. The two questions I most often ask students are "How did you get that?" and "Why did you do it that way?" Just getting the answer is not what is most important. The next time the answer will be different. What matters is the student's understanding of the process used to arrive at the answer so that the process can be refined, altered, or repeated for later problems. "I got that answer, but I'm not sure how" is not acceptable. In an atmosphere of constant questioning, students are forced to clarify their thought processes, analyze their errors, and refine their own questions.

By supporting and appreciating diversity of methods, we teach flexibility. Students who are required to do things in exactly one way will have difficulty dealing with ambiguity, finding alternative ways to solve any type of problem, or trying something when they are not sure what to do.

Math teachers are notorious for inflexibility because of their own learning styles and their belief that mathematics is an "exact" science. Yet we must be willing to model flexibility in many ways. In my classroom, flexibility has been one of the hardest things for some students to accept. For so long, students have been told to follow certain directions and to do it "just this way." They are often at a loss when I refuse to provide specific parameters. Certainly, some things are mathematically incorrect, but mathematics also encompasses much more flexibility and ambiguity than most of my students have been led to believe. If they are to survive in a constantly changing society, then they must appreciate and practice flexibility.

Appreciating flexibility does not preclude striving for excellence and producing high-quality work. In the fast-food, throwaway society of the

United States, students often don't gain an understanding of what constitutes high quality. Whenever we ask students to produce something—a
homework assignment, an essay question, a project—we must work to
develop their appreciation for and understanding of what a high-quality
product is. When we see positive changes in the quality of their work,
their writing, their questioning, and their responses, then we know they are
striving for higher levels of precision and accuracy.

Processing Experiences

Keeping a journal is often suggested as a way of supporting growth in students' thinking skills. Many times my students are surprised by the "writing" they have to do for math class, writing that begins on the first day! Yet
as time goes on, this journal time provides an opportunity for students to
be creative, thoughtful, and reflective. Some children find this time the
most rewarding part of my class.

The fact that they are given a grade based on their thoughtful completion of assignments each quarter reinforces the importance I place on
their thinking and writing. At first they don't believe I actually will read
their journals. When I return journals with supportive comments and specific feedback, students realize I am serious about their writing. When I
make comments in class about the feedback and suggestions they give
me—and then act accordingly—their ownership of the class increases, as
does their belief that they can make a difference.

Early in the year, I must be open and willing to accept whatever
responses I get. This approach also requires great flexibility on my part. I
remember one student in Algebra II who started the year quite sure that
he would never pass my class. He had barely passed Algebra I. During
the second week in school, I asked him to explain why a negative number times a negative number is a positive. He had not a clue. He did, however, respond quite creatively with a poem, which ended, "Why ask why,
ask why?" When he volunteered to read his response the next day, I
applauded his sense of humor and his creativity. He soon began to display
other intelligent behaviors, such as persistence and questioning. I am
happy to report he passed my class and went on to a four-year college,
intent on a degree in nursing.

Here are some examples of the types of questions I have given for journal assignments. They are not specifically math questions, but they support the processing of students' learning and provide me feedback about our class:

- "When I hear the word *math* I think _____ and I feel _____."
- "Problem solving means _____."
- "The hardest thing about problem solving is _____."
- "I took this course because _____."

Here are other examples of journal prompts and additional activities:

- Ask students to analyze a class activity: "What did you like and what did you not like about the activity? What did it help to clarify for you? What is still not clear?"
- After the first few cooperative learning activities, ask students what they did and did not like about them. For example, how did the group follow directions, work together, and communicate?
- To practice metacognition, ask students to explain some task or problem and how they thought it through.
- Ask students to think of a nonmath problem they've had in the last few months. Ask them to describe how they solved the problem and at least two other ways they could have solved it.
- Have students compare and contrast concepts learned. For example, after they've learned four methods for solving a system of linear equations, I might ask students to compare and contrast using the four methods. Which one seems the easiest or most efficient to them more often? Why do they seem to prefer one over the others?
- Ask students to propose criteria and their rationale for the evaluation of a project. Follow this work with a class discussion in which students must reach a decision on the criteria for grading.
- Ask students to describe which two Habits of Mind they display most often. In which two have they shown the most improvement? How and when do they display them? Which two do they have the most trouble using? How can they improve in these areas? In which two Habits of Mind do you, the teacher, most need to improve? Ask for suggestions of how you might work on those areas.

• As a review assignment, have students explain what concepts they should understand as a result of a unit. What should they be expected to know for a test? Have them create possible questions for a test.

• After they complete a project, ask students to evaluate it. What skills or concepts did they have to use? What did they learn from completing the project? What Habits of Mind did they have to use? How did they use them?

• When you try new things in the classroom, have your students give you feedback. Was the new strategy helpful to them? Why or why not? What suggestions do they have for making it better the next time?

• Ask students to use a Venn diagram for comparing and contrasting characteristics of themselves with two other family members.

• Before or after holidays or other big events (such as the prom), have students describe using Habits of Mind in that special situation.

• Have students analyze a test situation. Was the test what they expected? How did they prepare for the test? What should they do again or do differently next time?

• Ask students to create new Habits of Mind they feel should be practiced. Ask them to explain these habits.

Students' journals have provided me with some of the most accurate assessments of my teaching and of student learning. Sometimes students are painfully honest, especially after they know I will not hold their comments against them. Sometimes I agree with their assessments; other times I don't. For example, several years ago my honors students, who are mostly sophomores, had difficulty accepting some of my teaching practices. Because I did not tell them they had to do certain problems a certain way, they were confused by the ambiguity. Because I did not check their homework every day, they did not always do their assignments. As a result, many of them were not pleased by the grades they received. I even had a guidance counselor work with them one day so they could air their complaints.

When students realized I was not going to give in and accept responsibility for their lack of responsibility, they began to work harder. At the end of first semester, I asked them to consider what they needed to do differently in the second semester. I also asked them what I, as their teacher, and their parents could do to support them. Almost without exception, they said that we needed to encourage them, but they agreed that the responsibility for the learning was theirs.

Another way I have provided processing experiences for my students is through projects. I pose the following problem: "For your birthday I am going to give you a present: a big dog. In order for you to be ready, I am going to give you the material for a doghouse ahead of time. I'll give you one piece of plywood, four feet by eight feet, and some nails. You have a saw, a ruler, and a hammer. Your goal is to design and build (on paper) the biggest doghouse you can." We talk about the fact that they will need to define for themselves what constitutes a doghouse and how they will determine "the biggest."

On the day they bring in their projects, we have a class discussion to establish a definition for "doghouse" and how we will determine "the biggest." These discussions can become very heated! By the time we have finished our discussions and tried to determine the biggest, students are amazed by how much math and how many Habits of Mind they have used. Often, students comment in their reflective journals that next time they will think much longer when confronted by what seems to be an easy little assignment!

Thoughtful Decision Making

I am constantly appalled to find my students lack the knowledge of how to make a thoughtful decision. The problem, I suppose, is that the responsibility to teach decision-making skills does not fall under any specific curriculum. Many of my students are not taught those skills by their families, either. Several years ago, I decided I would not let my juniors and seniors graduate from high school without at least one formal experience in decision making.

Students may choose their own decision to make. Most work on choices for college or careers, but I also have had students decide when would be the best time to get married or what to buy someone for a present. Figure 10.1 shows the project as it is presented to students. The way in which they are to document later steps is discussed with them in class as we go through the project. Many students have told me through the years that this project was the most important thing they learned in my class.

Assessment

Assessment is another area in which I have experimented with my students. I have attempted to use a variety of formal test questions, including

FIGURE 10.1
Decision-Making Project

The Steps in the Process:

1. Define the problem. What decision do I have to make?
2. Identify areas of concern. What are my options? (This step often requires research.)
3. Predict consequences. List for each option the positive and negative possible outcomes. (This step usually requires research.)
4. Prioritize. What is the likelihood of that consequence occurring and how important is it to my decision?
5. Assess sources. How reliable is each source from which I received information? Is the information objective?
6. Make a decision. Based upon the information gathered, what is the best choice for you?

We will discuss each of the steps in the process during class. You will individually keep a record of the process for your own decision. At the end of the project, you will be expected to turn in a clear, well-organized presentation of the process you have completed. You will be graded on the evidence of the thoroughness of your process and the clarity of your presentation. Each step not completed and checked on time will result in a loss of 3 points per day late. The project will count as one test grade.

Step	Due Date
1. Decision to be made	November 17
2. List of options	November 21 and 29
3. Possible outcomes	December 1
4. Prioritize outcomes	December 6
5. Assessment of sources	December 6
6. Make a decision	December 9

Name: _____

Step 1. What decision do I have to make?
_____
_____

---

the type of open-ended questions that now are showing up in testing programs. The world outside school does not always function through multiple-choice or fill-in-the-blank tasks or evaluations. Students must experience, in the relative safety of the classroom, the unstructured, ill-defined problems they will encounter in life.

As I began to make so many changes in my teaching practices, I felt the need for some "hard" data about my progress. My end-of-course test scores have remained fairly stable, usually with a slight increase from year to year. Yet these were not the data for which I searched. Much of what I was doing was not assessed by state tests. Finally, I developed a student survey that I administered two years in a row. Students answered anonymously.

Although the hard data from the survey were encouraging, "soft" data like the following story warm my heart. Several years ago, one of my students, Rita, was in a minor car accident on the way to school. As she sat in the office waiting for her parents to arrive, the assistant principal tried to keep Rita's mind occupied by asking her about her classes and teachers. When Rita told her she was in my class, the principal asked how she felt about that. Her response was, "She makes you think so hard your head hurts!"

I have watched my own children go off to school filled with wonder and a joy of learning that I rarely see in my students. My vision, shared by many others, is to develop schools that nourish and support rather than stifle that wonder and joy. I often remind my Algebra II students about the limitations of their math knowledge. Just as a 1st grader may say you can't subtract 3 from 1, or a 3rd grader may say you can't divide 2 by 5, my students will tell me you can't divide by zero. My response is that's true with real numbers, but you'll come close in calculus. When they say there is no square root of -4, I agree that there is no real answer to the square root of a negative number; they will have to wait until second semester when we expand the world of real numbers to the complex numbers, which include imaginary numbers.

I want students to continually wonder about what still lies ahead on their learning journey. This idea was expressed best in a statement made by my minister: "As your island of knowledge grows, so grows your shoreline of wonder." Nurturing both knowledge and wonder is my role as a teacher; I happen to use mathematics as the vehicle to reach that goal.

11

An Integrated Approach to Teaching Habits of Mind

Nancy Skerritt and Emilie Hard

It has been estimated that 80 percent of the jobs available in the United States within 20 years will be cerebral and only 20 percent manual, the exact opposite of the ratio in 1900. A quadriplegic with good technical and communications skills is becoming a more valuable worker than an able-bodied person without those skills. . . . Minds will be preferred over muscle.

—Jennifer James
Columnist for The Seattle Times

The Tahoma School District in Maple Valley, Washington, has worked aggressively to align its curriculum, instruction, and assessment with the skills students will need to live and work in the 21st century. To this end, the district adopted a profile that names six student outcomes: they will become collaborative workers, complex thinkers, quality producers, effective communicators, self-directed learners, and community contributors.

As the district created structures to support teachers' and students' work with these outcomes, it quickly became apparent that the outcomes contained an inherent need for directly teaching thinking processes and habits. For example, collaborative workers are flexible and show empathy. Complex thinkers demonstrate metacognition and problem-solving abilities. Quality producers are deliberate, not impulsive. Effective communicators demonstrate fluency and precision in language. Self-directed learners are persistent and inquisitive. Community contributors often take risks.

Eventually, the district adopted a thinking skills curriculum that identifies 20 thinking processes and 12 thinking habits, adapted from the work of Arthur L. Costa. In Tahoma's work with the Habits of Mind, the ultimate goal is for students to internalize and use the habits, not merely to recognize them in others.

The Core Unit

Tahoma's curriculum has been written to intentionally incorporate direct instruction in thinking processes and habits. This work includes establishing unit outcomes and guiding questions, teaching introductory and application lessons, and then assessing students' application of thinking skills. The district has developed three core units at each grade level, kindergarten through 6th grade. (Work recently was completed on units at the secondary level.) These resources provide the structure for new and experienced teachers to help students acquire the characteristics described in the district's goals.

To show how Tahoma's curriculum weaves thinking habits throughout all classroom work, we highlight one of the core units: "Growth of a Nation." This unit is taught in 6th grade. Like all units, it begins with establishing an outcome and guiding questions, which provide focus and direction for both teacher and students. The following extract from the Tahoma School District Core Curriculum details this unit.

Growth of a Nation
Grade 6

Students will explore the Systems and Relationships that defined the growth of our nation during the Westward Movement and Civil War in order to develop the skills of Self-Directed Learners and Community Contributors in a democratic society.

1. What were the causes of the Westward Movement?
   - Storyboard timeline
   - Trappers/fur traders

- Homesteading
  - Oregon Trail
- Religious freedom
- Manifest Destiny
  - Impact on Native Americans
- Gold rush/wealth
- Outdoor classroom experiences

Teach *Cause and Effect* thinking skill

Teach *Persistence, Risk Taking,* and *Deliberativeness* thinking behaviors

Apply *Finding Evidence* thinking skill
- Tall tales
- Narrative writing
  - Logs/journals

2. What Systems and Relationships were evident before and during the Civil War?
- Issues leading up to the war:
  - Economic systems: agrarian South vs. industrial North
  - Social systems: human rights—slavery
  - Political systems: nation's vs. states' rights
- Relationships during the war:
  - Human rights: slavery/Underground Railroad
  - Major events of the war:
    - Famous battles and leaders
    - Gettysburg Address
    - Emancipation Proclamation

Apply *Point of View* and *Fact and Opinion* thinking skills

Apply *Empathy* thinking behavior

Reader's Workshop: historical fiction

Poetry Study: Langston Hughes

Civil War reports and presentations

3. How can we, as Americans living in a democracy, contribute to freedom and equality for all?
- Martin Luther King Jr.

- Human rights issues today
- Personal goal setting: *Self-Directed Learner/Community Contributor* service projects
- Multiple intelligences project menu
- Art mural project

The outcome statement clarifies a purpose for the unit. In this case, students study the Westward Movement and the Civil War to develop skills related to being self-directed learners and community contributors. The guiding questions help sequence the learnings and bring more specificity to the unit outline, including which thinking processes and habits are taught and applied.

Through the first guiding question, students explore the causes and effects of the Westward Movement. They apply the reading strategies of previewing, skimming, and summarizing as they find evidence for how early settlers demonstrated the habits of taking responsible risks, persisting, and managing impulsivity. Teachers challenge learners to consider what these habits look and sound like. Naming these indicators enables students to understand the thinking behaviors in more concrete ways.

Students also use the indicators to search for evidence of the thinking habits. For example, students might say that Lewis and Clark were risk takers when they explored unfamiliar land and encountered dangerous animals. Early missionaries were persistent because they endured in the face of numerous obstacles. Homesteaders were deliberate as they carefully planned and prepared supplies for their journey.

Students can explore the content and thinking habits further through skits that depict settlers using a habit. For example, one skit might show that homesteaders sometimes had to travel with complete strangers, which illustrates risk taking. Another skit might show Brigham Young managing impulsivity by sending people ahead to create stopping places, build shelters, plant crops, and mark the trail.

Students notice that lack of a thinking habit sometimes contributes to an unsuccessful pursuit. Consider the gold prospector who perished because he wasn't deliberate enough to plan for adequate supplies during his trip to California. In another lesson, students compare and contrast traditional Native American values about the land and its resources with their own values. They begin to set goals for the use of outdoor classroom sites, and they build on their experiences during the following lesson as they develop guidelines for exploring and enjoying nature (which also contributes to managing impulsivity). In the process, they examine their roles as community contributors.

Lessons intentionally provide for transfer of learnings to students' life experiences to make education more meaningful. As students reflect on times when they have been particularly persistent (perhaps when learning a sport or a skill) or times when they were risk takers (meeting new friends, moving to a new area, trying new foods), they see how these Habits of Mind affect them personally. They connect thinking habits and goal achievement, and they come to understand why these habits are desirable.

As seen in the extract, Guiding Questions 2 and 3 invite students to investigate the systems and relationships that were evident before, during, and after the Civil War. Empathy becomes the focus as students gain an in-depth understanding of Northern and Southern perspectives on slavery and human rights issues. Students examine the treatment of slaves, the Underground Railroad, and the Emancipation Proclamation. They also investigate contemporary human rights issues by studying the poetry of Langston Hughes and the civil rights movement in the 1950s and '60s. The overall goal is for students to acquire the habit of empathy as they consider the perspectives of diverse people within a culture, overcome any racial hatred or bigotry, and develop genuine concern for the welfare of others.

Empathy in All Grades

As mentioned earlier, "Growth of a Nation" is taught in 6th grade. But we can trace the teaching of one of the habits it encompasses, empathy, throughout a student's career. For example, empathy is taught in 1st grade with a lesson on the picture book *The Rainbow Fish* by Marcus Pfister. The beautiful fish in the story learns kindness and helpful actions by sharing his scales with the other fish. After reading the story, students discuss the characteristics of empathy: helping others with kind actions and words, caring about other people, being concerned about problems that others face, asking questions to show concern, and looking at others when talking. The children use this understanding to create a "Code of Cooperation" for their classroom so that empathy becomes part of the culture of their learning environment.

At Grade 2 in the South America unit, students revisit the characteristics of empathy in relation to the story of "The Great Kapok Tree" by Lynne Cherry. Questions that guide the discussion include the following:

• How do you know the man became empathic in the story?
• How and why did the man in the story develop empathy for the creatures of the rain forest?
• How did having empathy affect his actions and behaviors?
• Can you think of a time when you have felt empathy for an animal? Did this change your behavior or actions? How? Why?

In a 3rd grade unit on Africa, students explore folk tales. One of these is "Mufaro's Beautiful Daughters" by John Steptoe. Students evaluate which character in the story demonstrates the most empathy. Students also provide specific evidence for their choice.

A 4th grade unit on Asia has a lesson called "Cultural Contact." Students read *Encounter* by Jane Yolen to discuss cultural contact as depicted in the story. They examine the elements of the two cultures that are in conflict, and they identify the barriers that limit communication. Students explore how empathy is important when meeting people from different cultures. This concept is then transferred to exploring the diverse cultures of Asia. The children are challenged to consider their own experiences with cultural contact to expand point of view and develop sensitivity toward others.

In 5th grade, students conclude their study of the novel with *Number the Stars* by Louise Lowry. They are asked to find evidence of the Danish people's empathy toward others throughout the story. Students review the story elements of plot, character, setting, and theme as they list specific examples of empathy. Then students share how they can demonstrate empathy in their own lives, and they link empathy to the creation of a peaceful world. The children brainstorm ways to maintain peace among family members, school companions, or people in the community. They create a "Peace List" on a bulletin board and illustrate their ideas. Then they search for evidence of peacemaking acts in newspapers and magazines. As a class, they also create a "Peace Collage." This collage is a culmination of their study of the diverse cultures of Europe, and it reinforces the district goals of becoming effective communicators and collaborative workers.

Well-Grounded Students

By the time students work with empathy in 6th grade, they are well grounded in this thinking habit. As they begin "Growth of a Nation," they use dictionaries and thesauruses in an initial lesson to review empathy (see the template in Figure 11.1). They examine word parts to deepen understanding. They tell why it is important to have empathy for diverse

FIGURE 11.1
Defining *Empathy*

Recall what the word *empathy* means.
Use a dictionary to look up and record the definition of the word *empathy*. Include the origin of the word.
Use a thesaurus to look up synonyms for the word *empathy*.
Tell why it is important to have *empathy* for the diverse perspectives, cultural differences, and different challenges faced by people in our community.

Source: Excerpted from Tahoma School District Core Curriculum, Maple Valley, Washington.

FIGURE 11.2

Empathy Thinking Behavior Chart

List the behaviors that would demonstrate what *empathy* looks like.
List the behaviors that would demonstrate what *empathy* sounds like.

Source: Excerpted from Tahoma School District Core Curriculum, Maple Valley, Washington.

perspectives, cultural differences, and varying challenges faced by people in the community. Then students create their own "Empathy Thinking Behavior Chart," using a template that prompts them to list what empathy looks like and sounds like (see Figure 11.2, above). These activities build on past experience, challenge students to think at deeper levels of understanding, and create ownership for the learning.

This establishing lesson is followed by application of empathy to human rights issues during the Civil War. Students read *Sweet Clara and the Freedom Quilt* by Deborah Hopkinson. They use three more thinking behaviors to investigate Sweet Clara's character in the story: originality, persistence, and inquisitiveness. Students next discuss examples of empathy in the story. Students work in groups of four to create a collage that demonstrates empathy. They use magazine pictures; illustrations; and their own graphics, slogans, or labels to represent the concept of empathy. Finally, they use an empathy performance checklist to self-assess their progress in demonstrating empathetic behaviors (see Figure 11.3).

Students also weave empathy into selections about historical events from *War, Terrible War* by Joy Hakim. For example, students read about Lee's surrender to Grant and consider how each leader demonstrated empathy toward the other at this climactic event of the Civil War. Students are encouraged to model empathy as they role-play this scene. Finally, students reflect on what it means to live in a democracy by writing about the

FIGURE 11.3
A Checklist to Self-Assess Progress

Name: _____   Date: _____

Showing Sensitivity and Understanding Toward Others

EMPATHY PERFORMANCE CHECKLIST		
Indicators: I demonstrate these behaviors ...	**Yes**	**No**
Helpful Actions • Acts of kindness		
Attentive Listening • Paraphrasing • Spending time talking		
Concerned Expressions • Head nodding in agreement • Similar emotions		
Interested Questions • "Tell me more." • "I want to understand."		
Affirming Statements • "I understand." • "I care about you." • "I want to help you."		

Source: Excerpted from Tahoma School District Core Curriculum, Maple Valley, Washington.

core beliefs "all men are created equal" and all are entitled to "life, liberty, and the pursuit of happiness."

Many other Habits of Mind are woven into Guiding Questions 2 and 3. Students apply risk taking to an exploration of the Underground Railroad. They brainstorm characteristics of risk takers, apply these characteristics to Harriet Tubman, discuss how many people were risk takers in helping slaves to freedom, and reflect on risks they have taken in their own lives. Attending and persistence are applied to work students do in exploring major battles of the Civil War. Students practice the skill of skimming for information, complete a "Battle Matrix" with facts about major battles, and then self-evaluate their efforts with a performance checklist that incorporates expectations for demonstrating the two targeted Habits of Mind.

Guiding Question 2 culminates with a project entitled "The Civil War Hall of Fame." Students select one famous leader from a list that includes Abraham Lincoln, Robert E. Lee, Ulysses S. Grant, Harriet Beecher Stowe, Harriet Tubman, and Sojourner Truth. Students take notes, produce a written report, create a visual presentation, and give an oral presentation. An important component of the project is to identify three Habits of Mind that the Civil War leader demonstrates. This evidence provides the basis for nominating the person to the Civil War Hall of Fame.

The evaluation criteria for all aspects of the project are completely centered on the Habits of Mind. The students and the teacher evaluate each component of the assignment according to criteria connected to a specific habit. Note taking is linked to managing impulsivity and being inquisitive; the written report is judged for fluency, elaboration, and persistence; the visual presentation is connected to standards for originality and precision; and the oral presentation is linked to risk taking. Students use the Habits of Mind to assess their own performance, internalizing standards for personal achievement.

Figure 11.4 shows the scoring rubric used to evaluate the Civil War Hall of Fame project. The total score in each category is weighted so that the total possible points for the project equal 100. Teachers can then easily convert the project grade to a letter grade.

Habits of Mind are equally important in other subject areas. For example, efforts to integrate math content with core units has resulted in applications such as "Glenda Gold-digger." Students are presented with a gold prospector who needs to determine the amount and worth of the grams of gold in her collection. Teachers reinforce persistence as students use different approaches to the problem. Students use the habit of metacognition as they explain the steps in their strategies and reflect on the effectiveness of those strategies and the reasonableness of their solutions.

The Habits of Mind are woven extensively throughout all of Tahoma's units. The district strives to structure the acquisition of content through

FIGURE 11.4

Civil War Hall of Fame Scoring Rubric

Name: _____ Date: _____

Scoring Scale

4 = Exemplary 3 = Consistently 2 = Sometimes 1 = Rarely NS = Not Scorable

NOTE TAKING

Managing Impulsivity
Score: _____
- Intentionally sought and gathered essential information
- Used a variety of sources
- Accurately interpreted information

Inquisitiveness
Score: _____
- Displayed an enthusiasm for exploration and sought new learning
- Looked for additional information
- Made connections with past learning

Total score: _____ X 2 = _____

ORAL PRESENTATION

Risk Taking
Score: _____
- Demonstrated the ability to perform in front of a group by speaking clearly and using good eye contact
- Showed evidence of being comfortable by expressing information in an original way

Total score: _____ X 3 = _____

WRITTEN REPORT

Fluency
Score: _____
- Often showed evidence of a variety of ideas
- Clearly supported main ideas with sufficient information
- Showed evidence that ideas and concepts flowed together easily

Elaboration
Score: _____
- Demonstrated the use of multiple resources to develop own thinking
- Showed evidence of higher-level thinking process: analysis, synthesis, evaluation, and application
- Clarified thinking and added details

Persistence
Score: _____
- Effectively made attempts to communicate clearly by focusing on relevant information and clear organization
- Persevered at using correct mechanics
- Usually displayed an understanding of the importance of readability by having a legible report

Total score: _____ X 4 = _____

VISUAL PRESENTATION

Originality
Score: _____
- Created a unique product that showed evidence of taking risks and using unique approaches
- Showed interesting information about the subject

Precision
Score: _____
- Showed evidence of comparing work to criteria and checking for accuracy
- Displayed evidence of careful use of tools and materials

Total score: _____ X 3 = _____

Total points for project: _____ (100 points possible)

Source: Excerpted from Tahoma School District Core Curriculum, Maple Valley, Washington.

the lens of thinking strategies and habits as identified in the thinking skills curriculum. We use these habits and skills to enhance content learning, to promote connections to life experience, and to encourage self-reflection. Assessing the Habits of Mind is ongoing and embedded throughout the various lessons, as illustrated in several of the examples we have provided. In addition, we have developed instruction and assessment tools based on Costa and Kallick's notion that we must consider what it looks like and sounds like to demonstrate these habits.

Like students in many U.S. schools, Tahoma's students are accountable to state standards and are assessed on tests that require far more than the traditional recall of information. We are pleased that our schools have shown continued improvement in reading, writing, and mathematics as measured on these and other examinations. We believe that the emphasis we have placed on teaching thinking skills and habits is at the heart of our students' success. As Costa says, the true measure of success is not in knowing the right answer, but in knowing what to do when you don't know the answer. It is our belief that developing Habits of Mind will best equip our students for living and working in the 21st century.

12

Creating Thoughtful Readers
Through Habits of Mind

Rachel Billmeyer

The habits of a vigorous mind are formed in contending with difficulties.

—Abigail Adams

I want to improve my physical fitness so I will feel healthier and have better control of my weight. I think if I write a plan and monitor it daily I will stick with it. My plan will focus on two goals: to exercise on a regular basis and to cut out eating between meals and taking second portions at meals. My exercise goal will begin with walking a half hour twice a week and will increase to walking four times a week. Walking with a friend will hold me more accountable for getting out; I will ask Sue to join me. Keeping track of my progress in a fitness journal will be a good way of reflecting. I have read the information on exercise and healthy eating, have a positive attitude, and I tell myself I can exercise and control my weight.

How often have you heard comments of this nature or even said them yourself? People of all ages say they want to change some aspect of their lifestyle but have trouble accomplishing the task. Why is it so hard to alter behaviors? Health experts say it has to do with changing long-standing habits, established dispositions of the mind, some of which have roots early in life. Ultimately, habits reflect how one thinks about fitness, and to be successful with any regimen means changing habits of the mind. A common theme prevails in self-help or how-to-succeed books: develop productive habits of mind. A well-known model is presented in Stephen Covey's book *The Seven Habits of Highly Effective People* (1989).

Cultivating productive mental habits is a lifelong process. Changing behaviors requires a focus on habits such as managing impulsivity, communicating with clarity and precision, or remaining open to continuous learning. These habits not only affect personal behaviors and lifestyle; they also permeate educational settings that create and support literate environments.

Societal and economic changes as well as disheartening reading scores on standardized tests have caused schools to broadly emphasize literacy. Employability rests on the ability to read. For example, in 1974 auto technicians were responsible for 5,000 pages of print; in 1994 it increased to 500,000 pages; and by 2000 car mechanics needed to understand 1,000,000 pages of service manuals to fix an automobile. Students must be equipped with strategic reading competencies to navigate and succeed in this information age.

Educators lament that their students lack the requisite knowledge, skills, and mental dispositions to read and comprehend text. Teachers complain that students are not motivated to read. Yet teachers themselves often say they are too busy to read, and current research indicates that many upcoming teachers actually dislike reading. A shift in thinking must occur in which all educators focus on reading. It is time for teachers to examine their own reading habits, and, in regard to their students, not only to focus on young readers but also to give increased emphasis to the literacy needs of adolescents.

A common cure for attacking literacy deficiencies is the use of appropriate strategies. In an effort to focus classroom instruction on reading, districts are mandating that teachers use well-established reading strategies such as graphic organizers, the Frayer Model (Frayer, Frederick, & Klausmeier, 1969) vocabulary strategy, or Anticipation/Prediction Guides (Herber, 1978). Although reading strategies are helpful, *the engagement in reading is not the product of strategies alone but a fusion of strategies with mental dispositions.* Because reading is "thinking cued by text," readers create meaning by interacting mentally with the words on the page. Reading is more than simply moving one's eyes across the page of written symbols or word calling. The complex act of constructing meaning from text involves intellectual processes or dispositions that can be taught, learned, and optimized over time. For example, strategic readers know how to *think flexibly* and *persist* in order to better comprehend the text.

These intellectual processes or dispositions, frequently referred to as Habits of Mind, are emphasized in Art Costa's foreword for *Strategic Reading in the Content Areas: Practical Applications for Creating a Thinking Environment* (Billmeyer, 2004). He believes that through conscious use of Habits of Mind students will expand their capacities for reading more strategically in all content areas. Thus, the type of thinking emphasized coupled with a specific strategy has potential to develop strategic readers. The purpose of this chapter is to explain how Habits of Mind are integral to the development of strategic readers.

What Is a Strategic Reader?

Strategic readers are focused and in charge of their reading. They are aware of the mental dispositions necessary for comprehending a passage. Strategic readers know that reading has to make sense, so they develop a tool kit of formal and informal strategies to focus and monitor thinking before, during, and after reading. They are curious knowledge seekers who choose to read because they know reading opens doors of learning. *Specifically, a strategic reader works actively to construct meaning, is independent, and reads to learn.*

Which Habits of Mind Develop Strategic Readers?

Strategic readers possess and apply productive mental habits. They are aware of their thinking, feelings, and behaviors as they complete a task. They know how to manage, monitor, and modify their thought patterns. Art Costa suggests that all readers must develop three broad reading comprehension habits: self-managing, self-monitoring, and self-modifying (Billmeyer, 2004).

Strategic readers are self-managing. They approach their text as a form of problem solving; the problem is to create meaning from the text. They come to the task equipped with a purpose for reading, questions in mind, a flexible plan, data drawn from past experiences, anticipation of success, and creative alternatives for constructing meaning. Key Habits of Mind that help readers self-manage are *applying past knowledge to new situations* and *questioning and posing problems.*

Strategic readers are self-monitoring. Metacognition, thinking about one's own thinking, occurs when students are aware of what goes on in their minds as they read. They monitor their thinking before, during, and after reading. Strategic readers establish metacognitive strategies such as making connections to previous learning, visualizing scenarios, and comparing with other resources. They monitor their own comprehension, conscious not only of the meaning they are making but also of the adequacy of the processes they are employing to construct that meaning. Specific Habits of Mind that help readers self-monitor are *thinking about thinking* and *thinking and communicating with clarity and precision.*

Strategic readers are self-modifying. They reflect on, evaluate, analyze, and construct meaning. They are open to altering their perceptions, biases, and conclusions, and to synthesizing new learning and applying it to future activities, tasks, and challenges. Strategic readers view each reading task as a skill-building experience—an opportunity to continually evaluate and improve meaning. Specific Habits of Mind that help readers self-modify are *thinking interdependently* and *remaining open to continuous learning.*

Reading Strategies and Activities to Foster Habits of Mind

Each comprehensive habit is supported by specific Habits of Mind necessary for developing strategic readers. This chapter examines six key Habits of Mind and makes reference to other Habits of Mind as appropriate. The key habits are the following:

- Applying past knowledge to new situations
- Questioning and posing problems
- Thinking about thinking (metacognition)
- Thinking and communicating with clarity and precision
- Thinking interdependently
- Remaining open to continuous learning

Applying Past Knowledge to New Situations

The background knowledge of the reader greatly influences how the text is understood. Comprehension is a mental construction of what is on the page correlated with what is already known. The more knowledge a student has about a topic, the easier it is to derive meaning from new printed material on that topic.

Teachers should think of the prereading phase as an opportunity to give students a purpose for reading, to draw forth what is already known, to create interest, and to arouse curiosity. Johnston and Pearson (1982) believe that activating prior knowledge is a more accurate predictor of reading performance than IQ or test results. Because teachers are experts in their content areas and aware of what needs to be learned, they know which areas of prior knowledge should be activated to help students make the connections that will lead to understanding. For example, when approaching a reading selection on force in science, it is essential to have students draw upon what they know about mass and acceleration.

The gap between what students know and what the passage presents helps teachers determine what instruction is required during prereading. Sometimes students have misconceptions about the topic, and if teachers are aware of students' inadequacies, they can focus particular attention on those areas. Concepts can then be explored, clarified, and approached from different perspectives. Helping students compare the differences between their misconceptions and accurate information enhances retention and understanding. Prior knowledge can be organized into two categories: knowledge about the topic and related concepts, and knowledge about the vocabulary.

In addition to the often-used K-W-L (Know, Want to Know, Learned), two prereading strategies that focus on knowledge about the topic and related concepts are the Anticipation Guide (Herber, 1978) and the DRTA—Directed Reading/Thinking Activity (Moore, Readence, & Rickelman, 1982). Strategies such as these motivate readers and activate past knowledge.

The Anticipation Guide focuses attention on the major points of a concept to be studied. Before reading, students react to statements developed about the topic. The goal is to arouse students' curiosity by challenging their prior knowledge. The DRTA strategy asks students to record what they already know about the topic, what they are interested in learning, and finally, what they have learned about the topic during study. Whereas the Anticipation Guide is a teacher-directed strategy, the DRTA emphasizes student initiative. These strategies help the reader *apply past knowledge to new situations*. When teachers jump-start students' thinking before reading, comprehension increases. (Figure 12.1 shows examples of the use of these two strategies.)

Another type of prior knowledge focuses on vocabulary. It is important to help students make connections with critical terms related to the topic and to familiarize them with the meaning of words in new contexts. Comprehension improves when students are aware of critical vocabulary terms. Some teachers use the structure shown in Figure 12.2 to help students assess background knowledge about critical vocabulary terms.

Questioning and Posing Problems

> Students do not take responsibility for their comprehension when the teacher or the textbook is the "keeper of the questions."

Questioning is a powerful metacognitive tool to guide and monitor student learning. Self-questioning is one of the most potent cognitive tools for stimulating content learning; question generation prompts readers to search for answers that are of interest to them. The Question/Answer Relationships strategy (Raphael, 1986) is beneficial because it categorizes questions into four types: Right There, Think and Search, On My Own, and Author and You. Providing students with a cue card like that shown in Figure 12.3 supports their efforts with self-questioning.

The Enlighten Your Thinking strategy (Billmeyer, 2006b) offers a comprehensive list of questions developed for the 16 Habits of Mind. Questions can be used as an introduction to a lesson, during the lesson, or as a closure activity. Figure 12.4 shows sample questions for three of the habits.

When students learn how to access and build their own background knowledge, they become strategic readers. Struggling readers are often unaware of what they can bring to comprehending and learning from text. Frequently students are not aware of their own background knowledge and how they can use it to interact with the passage or to solve problems

FIGURE 12.1

Examples of Two Prereading Strategies

Anticipation Guide				
Topic: First Nation in Cyberspace				
Before You Read			**After You Read**	
Agree	Disagree		Agree	Disagree
_____	_____	1. The Internet, first developed by Paul Baran, was originally intended to be a military command-and-control system.	_____	_____
_____	_____	2. The Internet is now an uncontrolled electronic freeway that circles the globe.	_____	_____
_____	_____	3. Because the United States first developed the Internet, the U.S. government owns and maintains the Internet.	_____	_____
_____	_____	4. The Internet has no restrictions, meaning that anyone can say anything on it at any time.	_____	_____

DRTA—Directed Reading/Thinking Activity
Topic: Ancient Civilizations
What I Know I Know: Egypt is in North Africa. The Nile is the longest river in the world.
What I Think I Know: Egypt had pharaohs for their rulers. They built pyramids.
What I Think I Will Learn: How hieroglyphics were invented and how they were decoded.
What I Learned: The Rosetta Stone was key to deciphering.

when reading. Strategic readers, on the other hand, ask themselves these kinds of questions before reading:

- What do I know about the topic?
- What vocabulary is related to the topic?
- Which words or ideas might I encounter?
- What do I know about myself as I read this type of text?

FIGURE 12.2

Self-Assessment Tool for Vocabulary

Vocabulary Assessment—*Ancient Civilizations*			
Unknown— I have never seen this word.	**Familiar—**I have seen this word. I need to think about what it means.	**Recognized—** I automatically know what this word means.	**In-depth—**I have extensive knowledge about this word.
Platonic	*Pharaoh*	*Spartan*	*Hieroglyphics*

FIGURE 12.3

Cue Card for Students' Self-Questions

Right There—Literal Questions (who, when, where)

Think and Search—Interpretive Questions (draw conclusions, analyze, predict)

On My Own—Evaluative Questions (imagine, speculate, hypothesize, believe)

Author and You—Thinking Beyond Questions (interact, connect, associate)

FIGURE 12.4

Sample Questions Derived from Habits of Mind

Habit of Mind	Sample Questions
Applying past knowledge to new situations	*How does the passage relate to events or experiences you have had?* *How does knowing the findings of the scientist help you to understand the physical world?*
Questioning and posing problems	*What problems led the scientist to pursue experimentation?*
Thinking about thinking (metacognition)	*How did the author cause you to think? To feel?*

All students can learn how to think, reflect, and question in a competent manner. Questions linking content to a reader's life provide connections when learning factual information. Training all students to generate high-level questions helps all students learn how to think effectively before, during, and after reading. The goal of strategic reading is comprehension; strategic readers use the Habit of Mind *questioning and posing problems* to enhance understanding.

Thinking About Thinking (Metacognition)

Metacognition, or thinking about your own thinking, is at the heart of strategic reading. What we know today about strategic reading is a direct result of the research on metacognition.

Strategic readers use metacognitive strategies to facilitate active thinking and continuously check to see if they understand the author's message. Strategic readers are aware of their thinking as they read, selecting appropriate self-monitoring tools. When all students are strategic readers equipped with thinking about thinking strategies, reading in the content areas will be more productive.

The Think-Aloud (Davey, 1983) causes thinking, a covert process, to become overt. It explicitly helps students understand what goes on in the mind of the reader. For example, before reading a selection the teacher might say to the class, "As I preview this passage I am wondering what *enthymeme* means, and I'm thinking I better find out so the passage will make sense," or "I'm mulling over a prediction for this reading. I'm thinking it will be about three different rain forests and what makes them different." A benefit of the Think-Aloud strategy is that it helps students understand how the mind constructs meaning when reading as well as how it thinks through difficult spots. Figure 12.5 shows a Think-Aloud self-assessment guide and strategic reading journal.

To become a strategic reader means developing awareness of oneself as a reader and knowing fix-it strategies to solve problems that may occur when reading. Through direct teaching of the Habit of Mind *thinking about thinking*, students can become strategic readers.

Thinking and Communicating with Clarity and Precision

One of the biggest challenges in creating strategic readers is to teach students to *think about* and to engage in meaningful use of vocabulary. In her presentations, Heidi Hayes Jacobs (2006) has been heard to say, "If I were to do one thing to raise test scores, even on standardized tests, it

FIGURE 12.5

Think-Aloud Self-Assessment and Reading Journal

While I was reading, how much did I use these Think-Aloud strategies?	All the time	Quite often	Not much	Some	Very little
Forming a mental picture					
Connecting what I read to what I already know					
Creating new questions					

Strategic Reading Journal		
Before Reading: • Write down what you're trying to learn. • Brainstorm what you already know. • Predict what you think will happen. • Ask yourself a question.		
During Reading:	**Passage**	**Reactions**

• Use a sticky note to mark the places in the text that jump out at you, surprise you, connect you to something in the text, or tell about something you already know about.
• Jot your thinking on the sticky note so that you remember what your reaction was.
• Copy some of the passage so that you can refer to it.
• Note your reactions in the column next to the copied passage.
  ◦ This reminds me of ...
  ◦ I was thinking about ...
  ◦ This is like ...
  ◦ This explains why ...		

After Reading: • Answer the question you asked yourself in the beginning. • Summarize what happened or key points in a paragraph or an outline. • Tell why what happened is important.		

would be to build vocabulary. In chemistry, for example, students would write 'Dilute the solution with three milliliters of water' rather than simply, 'Add more water.'"

Vocabulary activities help students think and communicate with clarity and precision. Two examples of such activities are "word walls" and "words in the news."

Word walls. The saying "Out of sight, out of mind" highlights an important concept related to vocabulary development. Words need to be used at least six times before students internalize their meanings. Words can be displayed on a word wall to remind students to use them. Teachers and students record new or interesting words on butcher paper hung on the wall. Words can be organized into categories according to mathematical or scientific concepts, themes, origins, or letter patterns. Word walls provide quick and easy access for students during writing activities, when defining other words, or as a reference. Effective word walls are organized, placed at eye level, and highly readable.

Words in the news. A meaningful way to help students communicate with clarity and precision is to link vocabulary with current events. Teachers list the concept words from the text and ask students to make connections between the concept being studied and the current event (see Figure 12.6).

FIGURE 12.6
Linking Vocabulary with Current Events

Words in the News

Title and summary of the article: _____

Concept words:

empathy	physical systems	human systems
economic systems	nation-state	scarcity
citizen	culture	technology

I chose the word _____ because _____.

I chose the word _____ because _____.

Learning vocabulary words is a complex task. To gain and retain vocabulary words, students must listen to them being used multiple times, use the words as they speak, read them in context, and finally use them in meaningful writing activities. To become skilled users of new words, students will find that incorporating two Habits of Mind in particular—*persisting* and *taking responsible risks*—can pay big dividends.

Language is the visible edge of thinking. Observations, class discussions, interviews, and written surveys are methods used by teachers at all grade levels to determine students' habits and perceptions about themselves as readers. Surveys are beneficial because they alert readers to key elements of reading, and students can monitor how their attitudes and competencies change over time. Figure 12.7 presents examples of survey questions.

Survey results focus the teacher's perception of students' likes and dislikes, and competencies and deficiencies, thereby assisting in effective planning. Information can inform instruction in the following ways:

• Determine which books or sections of text to read aloud
• Determine supplemental reading material to be displayed in the classroom
• Guide individual students toward specific books, articles, or authors
• Determine which reading strategies to incorporate
• Share information with other teachers who instruct the same students
• Group students according to themes for projects or for Literature Circles
• Share information when planning with parents or guardians

Thinking Interdependently

When readers think interdependently, they are able to work with and learn from others in reciprocal situations. Learning and talking with classmates causes readers to be active composers of meaning. Collaborative work fosters positive interdependence. Not only is content stressed, but also all students are responsible for helping group members experience success with the assigned task. Numerous reading strategies cause students to *think interdependently*.

FIGURE 12.7
Student Reading Surveys

Open-Ended Response Statements

1. How would you describe yourself as a reader?

2. What are your favorite topics when reading? Why are they your favorites?

3. How do you feel when someone reads aloud to you?

4. How do you prepare yourself to read an assignment?

5. When you don't understand what you read, what strategies do you use?

6. If you were the teacher, how would you encourage students to read?

7. If you could change one thing about yourself as a reader, what would that be?

8. If someone gave you a $50 gift certificate from a bookstore, what would you buy?

9. Describe the place where you feel most comfortable and confident about your reading.

10. Why would you say reading is an important skill for life?

Short-Response Statements

	Always	Sometimes	Never
1. I like to read at home.			
2. I enjoy going to the library.			
3. I like to discuss what I read with my family or my friends.			
4. When I need information on a topic, I seek out reading material about it.			

FIGURE 12.8

Pairs Read Strategy

Read to Analyze

1. Determine the selection to be read with a partner.

2. Students work in pairs, with one student as the "reader" and the other assuming the role of the "coach."

3. The reader reads the first paragraph or section aloud to the coach. The length of each section to be read is determined by the difficulty of the selection. Students might stop in the middle of the paragraph to discuss complex ideas, asking "What's going on here?"

4. The reader summarizes the main idea of the section read. To push for analytical thinking, the coaching partner asks clarifying, probing, and inferential questions.

5. Students reverse roles and continue with the next section.

The Pairs Read strategy involves students reading aloud to each other, stopping to clarify ideas as needed, and then summarizing the information read. Figure 12.8 summarizes this strategy.

The L.E.T.S. Connect strategy (Billmeyer, 2006) engages the mind of the learner during a read-aloud or a video. Periodically the activity is stopped so paired learners can share with each other what they are thinking about the topic at that moment. L.E.T.S. Connect is an acronym with the following meaning:

L = Listen to the selection.

E = Engage with the content.

T = Think about the ideas and details, vocabulary, or sequence of events.

S = Say something to your partner about your thoughts.

Connect = Do all of the above steps and connect with the author, content, and other student's thoughts. Connections are any related thoughts that enter the listener's mind.

Although the L.E.T.S. Connect strategy emphasizes thinking interdependently, it also reinforces the Habit of Mind *listening with understanding and empathy*.

Discussion is a structured form of talking in which groups of students share their ideas to refine thinking and explore issues. Interactive discussions allow readers to closely examine a topic by exchanging understandings, ideas, and questions. Through dialogue students develop an awareness of their own beliefs and values about a topic. A sense of creative freedom evolves that encourages ownership of ideas and helps to build strategic readers. Two reading strategies that incorporate structured discussion are Reciprocal Teaching (Palinscar & Brown, 1984) and Literature Circles. Reciprocal Teaching is an interactive dialogue focusing on four reading attributes: predicting, clarifying, questioning, and summarizing. Students are organized into groups of four, with each student responsible for discussing one of the attributes. As students progress to the next paragraph or section in the selection, they rotate the reading skills.

Literature Circles encourage students to engage in and collaboratively process text. A Literature Circle is essentially a book club, a meeting in which people who are encountering the same text come together to discuss it. The best use of Literature Circles is when students are selecting texts they want to read, perhaps from a list predetermined by the teacher. Students assume roles to facilitate interdependent thinking; examples of roles are literary critic, conversation captain, and concept connector (Billmeyer, 2004). Strategic readers talk and *listen with understanding and empathy* to stimulate their thinking and to extend and refine their understanding of the content they have read. Strategies that cause readers to think interdependently not only create active minds but also deepen understanding of the selection read.

Remaining Open to Continuous Learning

Becoming a strategic reader is a lifelong process. If the goal is to create strategic readers who are independent, it is important that they exercise control of their own reading processes. Strategic control of the reading process means readers know and understand themselves as readers. For this to occur, students must establish one key Habit of Mind—*remaining open to continuous learning.*

An important reading attribute identified in *Capturing All of the Reader Through the Reading Assessment System* (Billmeyer, 2006a) is "Reflects on own reading process." Art Costa and Bena Kallick (2000) state, "To be reflective means to mentally wander through where you have been and to try to make some sense of it" (p. 61). For students to be able to transfer the use of strategies from one context to another, they need to reflect on how individual strategies assist comprehension. As teachers incorporate strategies, it is important that they help students understand how the strategy works and why it is effective in building comprehension.

Students then can use reflective feedback to construct meaning from text and to analyze themselves as readers. Reflective opportunities range from informal conversations between the teacher and the students ("What did you learn about yourself as a reader when using the anticipation guide strategy to study cell division?") to formal writing activities, such as writing a letter to summarize their learning or writing a letter to themselves citing insights they have gained as readers.

Journal writing is beneficial because it offers the reader time to reflect and project. When thinking is recorded, students gain a historical perspective of their work as well as an opportunity to plan. Some students find journal writing difficult; sentence stems can stimulate thinking and cause thoughtful reflection. Here are some examples of sentence stems for journal writing:

- What I learned about myself as I used this strategy . . .
- This strategy caused me to . . .
- I know how to adapt strategies when . . .
- When reading informative text . . .
- Ideas to remember about [topic] are . . .

The Write to Learn strategy (Billmeyer, 2006b) allows students to think critically, explore, and experiment with ideas, and to internalize content in a different way. Students are free to express personal ideas, concerns, and questions about the concepts they are learning. This unstructured writing encourages students to remain open to continuous learning. Teachers frequently use response journals, reading logs, or learning

FIGURE 12.9

Example of a Student's Response Journal for Science

Topic: Climate, Section 1-1

I developed the book questions but have these extra questions I'm interested in too.

- *Is CO_2 also in the air we breathe inside buildings?*

- *Since there is a rise in CO_2 will the food we eat be affected and toxify us?*

- *What is El Niño?*

- *As a scientist do you come up with everything yourself? What about the process of doing research and experiments?*

Topic: Climate, Section 2-1

This stuff on climate isn't half bad. Here are some things I learned. The climate is affected by two basic factors: temperature and precipitation. Latitude, elevation, and the presence of ocean currents are three factors of temperature, and prevailing winds and mountain ranges affect precipitation.

journals as tools for free writing. Figure 12.9 is an example of a response journal for science.

The development and monitoring of a personal reading plan, in which students set and reflect on personal reading goals, encourages students to focus on their own reading habits. Creating a personal reading plan also helps the reader develop the Habit of Mind of *persisting*. Writing a plan and implementing it are two different things. When students monitor and adjust their plans, they learn to persist and try another approach. Figure 12.10 shows the outline of a personal reading plan.

Strategic readers are never complacent about their level of performance. They always strive to learn more about their competencies, attitudes, and responsibilities as readers. Because reflection is not an inherent quality of most learning environments, it is important that teachers model habits of continual learning through reflection.

FIGURE 12.10
Personal Reading Plan

Name _____

Personal reading goals:

1.

2.

Steps to accomplish these reading goals (which Habits of Mind will be helpful?):

1.

2.

Reasons why these goals are important:

1.

2.

How Can Students Acquire Productive Habits of Mind?

Insanity is continuing to do the same thing over and over and expecting a different result.

—*Albert Einstein*

If Einstein's statement is true, then it seems evident that productive Habits of Mind need to be an integral part of the instructional process. Habits of Mind are alterable; people can learn to question, reflect, and think interdependently. Knowing and understanding productive mental habits encourages students to think about situations in different ways and to approach solutions with a greater probability of success.

Once students are knowledgeable about and skillful with Habits of Mind, they will become accustomed to asking themselves, "What Habits of Mind will help me to be successful in reading and understanding this material?" Changing a habit requires a conscious and conscientious effort on the part of the learner. Because nonexistent, underdeveloped, or self-defeating habits lead to poor learning, it is important to identify and teach specific mental dispositions. As teachers focus on content, it serves well to focus on Habits of Mind to increase student success. A clear, congruous correlation between course content and the Habits of Mind enhances learning of both.

Questions to consider when teaching the Habits of Mind include the following:

• Which concept or content requires the use of specific Habits of Mind? For example, success in mathematics depends upon *striving for accuracy*.

• Which habits will be introduced?

• Which habits need to be reinforced or emphasized?

• What is the best approach for teaching the habit? What real-life examples will help students understand?

• How will the Habit of Mind be reinforced?

• How might growth, refinement, and internalization of the Habit of Mind be monitored and evaluated?

Long-Term Goals

The complex act of constructing meaning from text involves Habits of Mind that are taught, learned, and optimized over time. The goal is to have students automatically employ these mental dispositions. A strategic reader, one who self-manages, self-monitors, and self-modifies, knows that mental habits influence thinking, comprehending, and learning. Just as monitoring food intake, nutrition, and exercise becomes a habit of a fit person, so does the use of Habits of Mind as they are embedded within reading strategies. As students experience success with these Habits of Mind, they will draw upon them when faced with challenging situations in reading and learning.

Teachers will discover countless ways to apply Habits of Mind to reading instruction. Just as these mental dispositions will support capable readers, so too will reading strengthen the habits and pave the way for their application throughout life. For this to occur, it is imperative that teachers consciously integrate Habits of Mind into their lessons. When the habits are intentionally taught, all students will have opportunities to acquire productive habits. A major goal of reading instruction must be to support students in developing and habituating these mental dispositions until the applications of Habits of Mind and the acts of comprehension are so interdependent as to be indistinguishable.

References

Billmeyer, R. (2004). *Strategic reading in the content areas: Practical applications for creating a thinking environment*. Omaha, NE: Rachel & Associates Inc.

Billmeyer, R. (2006a). *Capturing all of the reader through the reading assessment system: Practical applications for guiding strategic learners* (2nd ed.). Omaha, NE: Rachel & Associates Inc.

Billmeyer, R. (2006b). *Strategies to engage the mind of the learner: Creating strategic learners* (2nd ed.). Omaha, NE: Rachel & Associates Inc.

Costa, A., & Kallick, B. (2000). *Assessing and reporting habits of mind*. Alexandria, VA: ASCD.

Covey, S. R. (1989). *The seven habits of highly effective people*. New York: Simon and Schuster.

Davey, B. (1983). Think aloud: Modeling the cognitive processes of reading comprehension. *Journal of Reading, 27*(1), 44–47.

Frayer, D. A., Frederick, W. C., & Klausmeier, H. J. (1969). *A schema for testing the level of concept mastery* (Technical Report No. 16). Madison: University of Wisconsin Research and Development Center for Cognitive Learning.

Herber, H. (1978). *Teaching reading in content areas* (2nd ed.). Englewood Cliffs, NJ: Prentice-Hall.

Jacobs, H. H. (2006). *Active literacy across the curriculum*. Larchmont, NY: Eye on Education.

Johnston, P., & Pearson, D. (1982). *Prior knowledge, connectivity and the assessment of reading comprehension* (Technical Report No. 245). Champaign: University of Illinois, Center for the Study of Reading.

Moore, D. W., Readence, J. E., & Rickelman, R. J. (1982). *Rereading activities for content area reading and learning*. Newark, DE: International Reading Association.

Palinscar, A. S., & Brown, A. L. (1984). Reciprocal teaching of comprehension-fostering and comprehension-monitoring activities. *Cognition and Instruction, 1*(5), 117–175.

Raphael, T. E. (1986). Teaching question-answer relationships, revisited. *The Reading Teacher, 39*, 516–522.

13

Creating Curriculum with Healthy Habits of Mind at the Heart

Michael Goldfine

I believe that a curriculum centered on nurturing healthy mental habits will better help students succeed in school and in life. In this chapter I describe a successful eight-week-long poetry course that I have been developing over the course of 14 years to promote the Habits of Mind.

As a young teacher, if my class paid attention and looked engaged, I felt successful. In my first 10 years, it happened at times. Now, after 20 years, I look into the eyes of an individual student and ask myself, "Has she learned something today that really matters?"

What really matters is improved Habits of Mind. Will she be someone who, in the midst of chaos and crisis, objectively steps back, thoughtfully analyzes the roots and nature of the problem and the sequence of decisions to reorganize, engages others in reflective dialogue, and succeeds? What really matters to me is if my class work has helped her to use her mind and heart better.

Whether my current unit involves studying poetry, writing essays, experiencing *Hamlet*, or enjoying choice novels, I strive for learning that goes deeper than the acquisition of new skills and content. My eight-week poetry unit comes closest to achieving my ideals. After the unit, students readily recognize and acknowledge their ability to write better in all genres and especially appreciate the power of freewriting to more successfully mine their own creative depths, as well as respond to many life situations more boldly. I believe many of them, to different degrees, will approach all future academic challenges with more nerve and more consciously pursue better Habits of Mind.

In this unit, poetry is only the content vehicle. Discovering delight in reading and writing poetry is a secondary objective. The primary objectives are to help students more consciously and deliberately pursue the Habits of Mind, feel more creative and less fearful, write better, and be more adept at metaphorical thinking. At the end of the unit, I expect all of their prose to have more personality, use more imagery and metaphor, and be tighter, with a stronger sense of audience and purpose. I want to share my unit not as a recipe, but as an approach to creating curriculum with nurturing Habits of Mind at the heart.

Risk Taking and Dealing with Failure in a Healthy Way

In my poetry unit, I particularly focus on the Habit of Mind of *taking responsible risks* and a related habit not on Costa and Kallick's list: dealing with failure in a healthy way. I suspect the prime difference between people who are happy and feel successful and those who are dissatisfied with their life is that the happier people have dealt with their mistakes more thoughtfully. Everybody makes many mistakes. I wish we could look at mistakes as rough drafts or missteps. Those who are more dissatisfied in life are more likely to have rationalized their mistakes, perceived them less clearly, ignored them, or blamed them on others. But the successful take full responsibility and produce superior "drafts" next time.

Most likely everything you have achieved of great significance came from a risk you took in which failure was a real possibility. You can't have high-level successes without taking risk. Taking well-chosen intellectual and emotional risks is fundamental to rising to the next level. Dealing with failure in a healthy way is a fundamental habit that is very teachable, especially in conjunction with teaching the writing process. Revising creative works is a perfect simulation environment for learning to deal with weaknesses and strengths.

My college-prep seniors spend a lot of time in my class writing essays because that activity offers the greatest potential for gains in developing the Habits of Mind. Focusing, organizing, and developing a draft is an act of making meaning out of chaos. Using the language of the Habits of Mind to make that process more conscious for students raises metacognitive awareness. As I take them through the many required drafts, I am always reminding them, "Anybody can write well; it just takes hard work to improve each draft a little bit." And as I have students practice the drafting process again and again, I mention that all life is like an essay. Each day is a new draft—identify the strengths and build on them; identify the weaknesses and make them strengths. Then your life will get better and better.

Teaching Content Still Matters, but . . .

Content matters immensely, of course. Students still need to know about the Declaration of Independence, how to calculate without a computer, and about the process of photosynthesis. Some content is essential, but most content is not. Knowing how to dig in and learn well with a good attitude is essential. I believe secondary teachers are especially free to choose any good, relevant, complex, compelling content, but primary teachers are more restricted. I am not at all advocating getting rid of tests, lectures, all content-driven curriculum, or any traditional methods that get slandered by young, idealistic teachers and high-minded, scholarly theorists. All these methods have a place and can be useful in the proper balance. But exposure to all the great American authors will not help students succeed in college. However, being able to persevere, restrain impulsivity, and take a flexible approach to understanding challenging literature will help them succeed. Good curriculum driven by the Habits of Mind will teach academic skills as well as promote emotional intelligence.

An Overview of the Poetry Unit

The unit has three intertwined strands, each supporting the other like three strands braided into a rope that is 30 times as strong. In Strand 1, the students write 12 to 14 rough drafts of poems progressing from nonsensical wordplay, to open-ended highly structured forms like list poems, to less-structured forms, to fully open-ended assignments. In Strand 2, I dramatically read aloud or have them read a cornucopia of diverse poetry with an emphasis on what might appeal to young adults. In Strand 3, I teach a few select poetic devices, putting strong emphasis on practicing metaphorical thinking and writing with more imagery. At the end of the unit, I have them choose two of their poems, and we begin a revision process, culminating in a house reading party.

Strand 1: Writing Poetry and Promoting Creativity

Strand 1 is the heart of the unit. I use various opening activities to nurture a safe environment in which students can explore their creative selves. I deeply believe that all students are creative, but many have lost touch with their creative spirit because of fear. So the first thing I do is have them experience freewriting in various degrees of conscious abandonment. Freewriting is a powerful tool to help them bypass their conscious fears and self-editing urges and to draw from their deeper selves. Freewriting is a great way to begin almost any creative endeavor. I talk about how freewriting is a way of tapping into our deeper selves, the source of individual creativity.

Athletes need to stretch before a demanding burst of activity. I see my students as intellectual athletes, myself as the coach, and the classroom as a playing field. I start stretching with wordplay and have them write 20 three-word combinations, each word beginning with the letter that corresponds to their initial. For example, using my initials, MFG, I might brainstorm

- Monkey Finds Grapes
- Moron Feeds Gorillas
- Mr. Fish Groans
- Mustard Frozen Gorgonzola

We do some wordplay in class as a group and individually. They do some for Habits of Mind work—the best way to learn the Habits of Mind is to practice them again and again in different contexts, exercising the mental muscles—and we have fun sharing the next day. The wordplay provides some gentle mental stretching and helps create a safe, fun environment, which is essential to the bigger personal risks I intend to ask of students.

In another prewriting exercise to loosen and stretch, I give the students a simple sentence such as "I drove the car to the store" and ask them to rewrite it in 14 more interesting versions:

- I rode my rocket ship to the moon.
- I steered my Harley Davidson through the school's cafeteria.
- I drove my '64 Chevy pickup to Betty's beauty parlor.
- Putting the pedal to the metal, I raced my cousins to Pete's Bowling Alley.

The first poem I ask students to write is a "chant poem." I discuss the power of repetition in writing and song and the importance of variation after establishing a pattern. As with most of the poem assignments to come, I read the best examples from past years to inspire and excite. (Originally I used examples from books or wrote them myself.) Then I assign a chant poem for Habits of Mind work. After I collect the poems the next day, I select a half dozen of the most interesting and read them aloud, keeping the creators anonymous.

Often when students hear their rough, brainstormed effort read aloud anonymously, they are surprised by how promising it is and gain great confidence in their ability to create and improvise. In addition, students are noticing that the more interesting brainstorm efforts are often more honest and more personal and that there are endless possibilities for self-expression.

What is important in these poem-writing exercises is not writing good poems, but becoming comfortable with taking risks and trying different styles and voices. Above all, I want students to connect with their creative spirits and be comfortable with writing a lot of junk in order to write well. Besides exercising their imaginations, I think they strengthen other Habits of Mind: *applying past knowledge*; *gathering data through all senses*; *creating, imagining, innovating*; and some not covered by the list.

The fourth assignment and second poem is a "list poem." Along with student examples I read some examples from the likes of Walt Whitman and Gary Snyder. I want the students to have lots of room to be themselves—depressed, wild, goofy, or introspective—but not overly stressed by the pressure to create form and content. Offering these highly structured but open-ended assignments and being almost totally nonjudgmental in evaluation allows the students to feel more at ease in creating and improvising. The list poem usually works so well that I assign it a second time. The second time I vary it by having them walk somewhere and list at least

15 images they see, then spin a draft of a poem from their list. At some point, after a second and third lesson on imagery, I ask students to redo one of their poems, replacing generalities with specifics.

From the beginning, I invite students to break any of the assignment guidelines if their draft poem wants to go in a different direction. They rarely do, but it is important for them to know they don't have to follow the assignment guidelines. But they do have to write something. In the beginning, when we practice freewriting, I use a number of analogies, such as successful gold miners spending many days finding nothing and many more days finding only flakes in order to find one beautiful nugget here and there. Feeling comfortable in creating a lot of junk is essential to finding the creative self.

I continue with a poem assignment about place, a letter poem, a haiku assignment, a poem modeled on Alan Ginsberg's "Howl," and a poem modeled on Walt Whitman's "Song of Myself." Most students end up with at least several drafts that they are delighted and surprised by. In every class, a couple of students blossom and are blindsided by how well they write.

For the last couple of assignments, I offer no stimulus or suggested structure and simply ask for a draft of a poem the next day. They are now comfortable with that assignment. Six weeks earlier, if I had asked for a poem, I would have faced mutiny. Gradually increasing the complexity of the risks involved with writing drafts of poems nurtures risk taking. We overtly discuss the Habits of Mind. The students see their importance and appreciate gaining the language to help them become more conscious of their Habits of Mind.

In Strand 1, I am only getting through two, maybe three poem-writing assignments each week because Strand 2 and Strand 3 are going on concurrently.

Strand 2: Practicing Metaphorical Thinking and Writing with Imagery

Over the years, as I have taught many traditional poetic devices, I have come to agree with Aristotle, who said in *Poetics*, "But the greatest thing by far is to be a master of the metaphor." All poetic devices are types of metaphor. I would strongly argue that the bulwark of all high-level, abstract thought is metaphorical thinking. And the heart of reading and writing poetry is the pursuit of metaphorical understanding. I have a repertoire of exercises to promote metaphorical thinking. The exercises are a workout for the imagination. I also spend a lot of time with metaphor's prodigal daughter, imagery, using more specific detail.

I have found that generally depth rather than breadth more deeply nurtures Habits of Mind. So although I do one mini-lesson on sound devices, symbolism, and free verse versus traditional verse, I incorporate many exercises on thinking metaphorically and writing with more imagery, both of which are worthy of deep coverage.

Here is an example of an exercise I spend two periods on that helps the students to be more comfortable with metaphorical thinking. I bring in a box full of household items like toothpaste, a fork, a dog bone, a candle, a sponge, a light bulb, a screwdriver, a rubber duck, and so on. I pull out an object and have them brainstorm multiple comparisons between the object and our brain. We briefly unpack their metaphors. Then I have each student blindly pull an item from the box and create a metaphor between whatever item they pick and the concept of "knowledge." We share their metaphors. Many are funny, clever, and surprising, which generates a lot of student enthusiasm. Then they pick another item from the box and create a metaphor related to one of seven concepts I put on the board—such as Saturday night, religion, Michael Jordan, history class, Monday morning. Students generate metaphors such as these (which are actually similes—a simple form of metaphor): "Saturday night is like a dog bone because you are excited to start chewing on it," or "History class is like a screwdriver because it helps construct a house of knowledge."

Another exercise uses *synthesesia*, a type of metaphor in which an image from one sense is described in terms of another, such as "a cathedral is frozen music." I give the students something new to taste, like carob chips or sugared ginger, and ask them to describe the new taste using a visual, an auditory, a tactile, and an olfactory image. Then I do the same with a novel piece of music, a bristly brush to touch, cardamom to smell, and a violet piece of paper, each time asking for four metaphors using the other senses.

In class I often bring up the relevancy of schoolwork, and I find myself defending the importance of having math class every school day, every year. The gist of my argument is this: "It doesn't matter whether you ever use the specific math later in life. Doing math trains you to be more logical, systematic, a better manipulator of quantitative information, and a problem solver through trial and error—all vital Habits of Mind." Likewise, the work we do with poetry is training students to bring poetic sensibilities and skills to all of their endeavors.

Early in the unit, I introduce the importance of writing with more specific details in order to create imagery. Teachers often teach "show versus tell," but writing without imagery is painting without color, and so imagery deserves and needs great attention. I show how imagery often communicates more powerfully than generalities, entertains better, and often connects with a reader in a deeper psychological way, re-creating the experience so the reader can participate rather than just observe. After the initial lesson and several exercises, I come back to imagery again and again throughout the eight-week unit. I point it out in the poetry we read and the student examples. I gently ask students to push for imagery in the poems they are writing. I bring it up very deliberately later in the year when we write personal narratives and whenever other opportunities arise. At the end of the unit, we read Tim O'Brien's brilliantly written short story about the Vietnam War, "The Things They Carried," and notice how metaphors and imagery take the story to the highest literary level. When my students are 30 years old, sitting with friends around the dinner table telling the story about the time they stepped on a teddy bear cholla cactus, I expect their listeners to feel each cactus spike being pulled out of their own feet.

Strand 3: Hearing a Diverse Cornucopia of Poetry Read Aloud

Many teachers have learned that hearing poetry read aloud engages audiences more powerfully than if poetry is read silently. As my students generate many rough drafts of poems and practice metaphorical thinking and learning to write with more imagery, I read their poems aloud. Eventually, I invite them to pick and read poems.

In the first days of class, I know most of my students have learned to dislike poetry in school. Every year I listen to groans and moans when I say we are going to do poetry for eight weeks—knowing most of them will wander over and succumb to its delights. Most have a very limited idea of poetry. They often think of it as intimidating, unintelligible puzzles. So I dramatically begin reading poems such as Lucille Clifton's "Habits of Mindage to My Hips," Alan Ginsburg's "Sunflower Sutra," Marge Piercy's "Wrong Monday," and then run the gamut from hip-hop rhyme to Sylvia Plath over the course of the first five weeks. In the last few weeks, their poetry drafts take over the classroom airwaves.

It is essential that the students enjoy the poems and find many of them stimulating, or many of the benefits I'm seeking will not occur. What I am hoping to accomplish is to share the delight and beauty of interesting language that can ignite students' imaginations with endless possibilities for creativity. But I could live with them simply discovering that poetry is pretty cool.

Creating a Sturdy Rope from Three Interwoven Strands

Reading poetry has informed and inspired my students' writing. Writing poetry has informed their reading. And extended studies of metaphor and imagery have improved them as writers and thinkers.

Generating a lot of raw material has involved them in *taking responsible risks* and has provided many opportunities for *creating, imagining, and innovating.* Teaching the writing and revision process offers abundant opportunities to promote other Habits of Mind as well, especially those related to dealing with weaknesses and strengths in a healthy way.

Revising Two of the Poetry Drafts

I have the students keep all their poetry drafts in a writing folder. I ask them to pick two drafts—those with the most potential—to revise and read aloud to the class. I find time to confer with each student about the choices because I feel strongly about wanting them to succeed and feel good about their work.

Teaching students how to revise their work is a great vehicle to promote the Habits of Mind. Writing well is revising well. Producing at least half a dozen drafts is practicing *persistence.* Critiquing each other's drafts involves practicing *listening with understanding and empathy.* Working hard to get 50 words just right is likely to involve practicing *striving for accuracy and precision*. And above all, learning to identify the weaknesses and strengths of a draft, and then fortifying the weaknesses and building on the strengths is practicing the same kind of metacognitive awareness they should bring to all of life.

Some of the students are not happy about reading one of their poems to the whole class. Some are fearful of looking foolish. I deal with this with great sensitivity and occasionally make exceptions to the requirement. However, having a real audience with a real purpose is critical to maximizing the learning they gain from the unit.

During the last few weeks, I do a series of mini-lessons on revision skills related to such things as focus, audience, economy of language, line breaks, verbs, and word choices. With the exception of the lesson on line breaks, all the mini-lessons are just as pertinent to all forms of prose writing and speaking as they are to poetry. Practice in the Habits of Mind is my primary goal, but the inevitable by-products for students are that they become better writers and better users of language, and they are better able to succeed in college as a result.

Language and Life

At the end of the eight weeks, the relationship between language and life has emerged. The richness of the poetry has evoked much of the splendor and struggle of the students' lives. Having a better sense of audience, using imagery and metaphor, and tightening their language will improve all of their writing. But above all, my students have learned to take risks and to bring a more vital, creative spirit to living. As the story says, give a man a fish and he eats for a day; give a man a fishing rod and he eats for a lifetime. Nurture the Habits of Mind in your students and they will help you fix your fishing rod.

More and more, my former students return to visit and reassure me that curriculum built on the Habits of Mind has been better than the usual fishing. Readers may e-mail me at mfg12@scasd.org for more information about any of these ideas and activities.

14

Notes from the Gym:
Using Habits of Mind
to Develop Mind and Body

Marjorie Martinez

I work in Furr High School in Houston, Texas. The student profile at the school is African American, 20 percent; Asian, 1 percent; Hispanic, 76 percent; and white, 3 percent. Eighty-seven percent of the students qualify for free and reduced lunch, 76 percent are identified as "at risk," and 16 percent are limited English proficient (LEP).

In addition to the comprehensive high school, we have a charter school called REACH that provides a special program for students at risk. REACH has a high percentage of dropouts, and most of our students are three to four years below grade level. The students typically have low self-esteem, display a confrontational set of behaviors, are gang members, and have high rates of drug abuse and teenage pregnancy. I decided to focus on the habits with this group of students first.

I was introduced to the Habits of Mind, and I liked the structure they would provide for our kids. Like a nutrition or fitness plan, the habits would provide a sense of ownership and success at a faster pace because the concept would give them a framework for setting goals. The habits hold the kids accountable for their behavior, and they can see the immediate results when they are using the habits. The habits help them to make better decisions. The structure means that they have a plan—they have a way of organizing their thoughts for success.

As I began to plan how to use the Habits of Mind, my essential question was this: How can I implement this in physical education so that the students can take these habits outside this setting and become lifelong learners?

Introducing the Habits

I approached the introduction of the habits with three ideas in mind:

• Mastery of the Habits of the Mind would occur through experience, so that the students would assume ownership and experience success inside and outside the classroom.

• The approach to the program would focus first on getting the students engaged in practicing the habits through fitness activities while learning health concepts.

• The approach to the program would then use physical education as the setting for motivation and reinforcement of the Habits of Mind.

The students in Project REACH need a structure. I started by asking the students to evaluate their old habits—identifying why they were in a program like REACH and what the habits were that seemed to have brought them there. I then talked with them about managing impulsivity and persisting. We talked about how they had been put down, and we discussed the many confrontations they had had with police officers and teachers.

I then introduced the Habits of Mind. In my first round with the habits, I had some false starts. For example, I discovered that 16 habits were too many to introduce at one time. I discovered that students needed to take time to think about each habit and process what it would mean for them. I had to effectively structure the pace of introducing the habits to the students so that they would have some success in practicing use of each habit.

I selected the following Habits of Mind to create a foundation that fit with the students' ability levels and needs:

• Persisting
• Managing impulsivity

- Listening with understanding and empathy
- Thinking interdependently
- Metacognition
- Gathering data through all senses
- Taking responsible risks
- Remaining open to continuous learning
- Questioning and posing problems

I then prioritized the order of introduction of each habit to maximize the likelihood of each building the foundation for the next. The habits created a learning environment in which it was OK to take risks and ask questions. As students gained confidence, they started to come to class better prepared for learning. I started to think, if I can get them to do it for me in a physical education setting, imagine what they could do in other classes—and the success they would have.

I developed a cross-curricular focus in which we learned that physical education is not just about exercise or team sports. It includes everything that you do in any classroom: assessment, analysis, use of strategies, measurement, documentation, and decision making using data. In other words, I was able to develop cross-curricular expectations and communicate them to the students so that they would establish some accountability and ownership of their behaviors as learners.

The key ingredient that helped bring the students along was my ability to establish a positive rapport with mutual trust. I had a strong relationship with each student. I reinforced the behaviors that would show that the students were using the habits, such as good attendance, organization of materials, being prepared to work, and being punctual. I held the students accountable and responsible for their actions or lack thereof.

I started with journaling—I wanted the students to become more aware of themselves and their thinking. I wanted them to use the habit of metacognition—thinking about their thinking. The students needed to learn how to question, make decisions, and ultimately evaluate their decision making. An unexpected outcome was that through journaling I also identified writing deficiencies and used cross-curriculum strategies and developed activities to improve literacy skills.

Integrating the Habits into Physical Fitness Classes

The following are some examples of exercises I used to integrate the Habits of Mind into my physical fitness classes (related habits are shown in parentheses):

• Abdominal exercises require students to manage both their minds and bodies to ensure correct execution and to gain the desired benefits. Students have to persist so that they can work through the pain and avoid the natural impulse to quit. (*Managing impulsivity, persisting*)

• Students sit with their arms extended to their sides. Each student has to count in Spanish one by one. If a student does not know the correct number, the student is allowed to yell "help." Someone gives the answer and the student repeats the answer before the next person takes a turn. If a student doesn't yell "help" or someone just blurts out the answer, the student has to start counting all over again. (*Managing impulsivity, persisting*)

• In a sensitivity training exercise, students are blindfolded and work in pairs to play a game. They gain empathy for people with a visual impairment and realize that without each other's help, they couldn't play the game. (*Having empathy, thinking interdependently*)

• In playing basketball, students use their nondominant hand to perform the skills they typically do with their dominant hand. They have to stop and think and realize what is involved in the process so that they can perform it with the other (nondominant) hand. (*Metacognition*)

• Students gain confidence in asking questions by being encouraged to do so in physical education class. They need to be encouraged to do the same in, for example, algebra class. (*Questioning and posing problems*)

• As students work with weights in weight-training exercises, they must increase the intensity of the pace either in the hold or the push position. The students work in pairs, so that they can encourage and coach each other. Students come to realize that no matter how hard it gets, they can succeed. (*Persisting, thinking interdependently*)

• In the "hike to the hill" exercise, the goal is for students to hike to the top of a hill using already existing paths that are well worn or paths they create. Students then reflect on the experience and create a journal entry. (*Gathering data through all senses*)

• Students must evaluate their decision making in such areas as drugs, pregnancy, and alcohol by considering, for example, why they would get into a car with someone under the influence of drugs or alcohol. (*Taking responsible risks*)

• By using *any* situation to create a learning environment, students are exposed to as much learning as possible. (*Remaining open to continuous learning*)

The following suggestions apply to all the exercises I use:

• Have students maintain a journal to record reflections about an activity and their feelings.

• Work on students' literacy skills.

• Have students take responsibility for checking their binders and learning logs, which include a list of the habits. They have to continuously be reminded about the habits.

• Integrate and apply the habits in increasingly more difficult situations.

• Plan for students to be able to be successful and, at the same time, control for increasing the difficulty of the activity.

• Use analogies to reinforce the principles of the exercises and the use of the habits. For example, in weight training I ask students, "What are the weights that you hold?" to get them to describe difficult things they might be dealing with in life. On the hike to the hill I ask, "What path do you choose to get to the top of the hill?" to get them to think about the choices they make.

Our work follows a structured schedule. We focus on journaling every Monday, Wednesday, and Friday. We focus on physical fitness and health activities with reflective journaling on Tuesday and Thursday. We set a standard for good performance and eliminate any excuses for poor performance. Here are a few examples from student journals:

This exercise showed me that I can be a more effective listener. By Alejaraara and I sitting back-to-back, I could picture her brother hitting her for no reason. By listening to her I learned that she has a reason for being apathetic at times and lonely. —Dasha

When my partner, Sierra, and I hooked up, she listened to me and understood what I felt. This activity made me realize I could be a better listener because now I can hear what the person is going through without cutting them off. This can also help me with my parents. My mom is single and works hard. She is always persistent about my cleaning the house. Sometimes I get mad because I wasn't allowed to go out with my friends. Now I will listen to her and understand how she feels by being a good listener. I will think real hard and obey my mom. — Mojo

The exercise we did today was different from a regular gym class. We didn't do push ups or sit ups, but we did something even harder — "learning how to listen." Of course, class does some along with the physical work, but this is teaching us valuable lessons. I really like this class because it prepares us for the future. I don't even have to come to this class because I'm a senior and I have enough P.E. credits. But I do come because I will either be intellectually or physically challenged and that is what we need for our adult lives. — Julisa

Payoffs for Teacher and Students

Using the habits has made me more aware of myself, allowing me to enjoy my profession and my life more. I am always looking for new ideas and am continuously learning, thereby resisting complacency.

The students have benefited as well. Starting with 46 at-risk students in a two-year program, Project REACH graduated 15 of them (33 percent) at the end of the first year. An additional 12 students (46 percent) were scheduled to graduate at the end of the second year. Together, that equals an overall graduation rate of 59 percent for that cohort of students in Project REACH.

15

Cognitive Composition: Thinking-Based Writing

Rebecca Reagan

> Who can say what ignites a certain combination of words, causing them to explode in the mind? ... These are high mysteries ... there is no satisfactory explanation of style, no infallible guide to good writing, no assurance that a person who thinks clearly will be able to write clearly, no key that unlocks the door, no inflexible rule by which the young writer may shape his course. He will often find himself steering by stars that are disturbingly in motion.
>
> —*E. B. White*

The most formidable opponent to the writing process is the blank page. The expectation that it will be filled with intelligent prose or poetry weighs heavily on the writer, no matter what age. The result of the process is often a disorganized and superficial product. How can we as educators unlock the door to good writing? Where are the keys?

I seem to have spent most of my life looking for keys to one thing or another. Keys to skillful teaching, to appropriate student behavior, to classroom organization, . . . to the car. As a teacher of reading and writing, most often I have searched for the keys to teaching students how to read insightfully and to write carefully and intelligently.

There are three basic ideas or concepts that, when forged together, mold the keys to such writing. One is that *deep and careful thinking before, as well as during, writing is necessary for deep and careful writing.* The second idea is that such deep and careful thinking—what my colleagues and I call "skillful thinking" (Swartz, Costa, Beyer, Reagan, & Kallick, 2007)—needs to include both *the exercise of thinking skills and the use of relevant Habits of Mind.* And the third concept is that *the most effective way that skillful thinking can result in such deep and careful writing is through the use of "writing maps"* as part of thoughtful engagement by the students in the "standard" stages of the writing process: prewriting, drafting, editing and revising, rewriting, and the creation of a final product. The yield of all this—what I call "cognitive composition"—is an example of the implementation of *Thinking-Based Learning* (see Swartz et al., 2007). These elements together form the magical key that opens the door to one of the most powerful approaches to teaching writing.

Cognition, according to the *American Heritage Dictionary,* means "the mental faculty of knowing, which includes perceiving, recognizing, conceiving, judging, reasoning, and imagining." Random House defines *composition* as "the art of putting words and sentences together in accordance with rules of grammar and rhetoric." Cognitive composition, therefore, would be using our full mental faculties to put words and sentences together for effective communication. In other words, cognitive composition involves the engagement of skillful thinking to guide the composition of a piece of writing. It is in this context that appropriate and productive Habits of Mind dramatically facilitate the writing process by enriching our awareness of and engagement with audience, purpose, content, process, and product as we think and write.

The best way to demonstrate how this approach works is to provide a window into a classroom where instruction in skillful thinking, including Habits of Mind, and its extension into the writing process share equal space. Then we shall see if the keys open the door to good writing.

There are many kinds of writing. Each has its own character and requirements. Each has a variety of purposes and targets different audiences. Lessons in which instruction in skillful thinking is infused into content instruction will often lend themselves to a particular writing composition that can challenge students to transform the thinking they do into effective writing. The lessons that are described in this chapter bring out this connection and are referenced by the type of skillful thinking that is taught. Emphasized in each lesson are specific appropriate Habits of Mind that enhance the use of the skillful thinking strategy being taught and its extension into actual writing.

Comparing and Contrasting

My students have had difficulty producing quality compare/contrast essays. The most glaring problems involved not only the organization of the writing itself but also the use of inaccurate data and unimportant details. We were studying the English settlement of the New World in American history. When students compared and contrasted different settlements using just the basic questions of "How are they alike?" and "How are they different?" the results were less than stellar. As we read about Pocahontas and John Smith, for example, the students had problems separating fact from fiction, citing characters and events from the Disney version, and they tended to include only immediately apparent and hence often superficial similarities and differences.

I decided that this was an opportune time to look at actual history and Disney's Pocahontas, comparing and contrasting fact and fiction. It would also be a good occasion to introduce students to procedures for more skillful comparing and contrasting, while at the same time emphasizing key Habits of Mind that would enhance this process. One of the most readable nonfiction accounts about this historical period that has been published is *The Double Life of Pocahontas* by Jean Fritz (1987). I had obtained multiple copies of Fritz's book and asked students to read the first 25 pages, which led us to the famous event in which Pocahontas saved the life of John Smith. (Interestingly, many students continued to read the entire book.) Students then watched the Disney movie version of Pocahontas again. They were asked to take notes about the characters, setting, plot, and events that were depicted in the movie. As we had previously worked on how to extract precise details from a text with accuracy, the students were asked to employ those skills in their note taking.

We then thought about the strategy that we would use to compare and contrast the real version and Disney's—a strategy that would be more skillful than if we just made a quick pass at listing some similarities and

Thinking Strategy Map for Skillful Comparing and Contrasting

1. How are they similar?

2. How are they different?

3. What similarities and differences seem significant?

4. What categories or patterns do you see in the significant similarities and differences?

5. What interpretation or conclusion is suggested by the significant similarities and differences?

From *Infusing the Teaching of Critical and Creative Thinking into Content Instruction: A Lesson Design Handbook for the Elementary Grades* © 1994 The Critical Thinking Co. www.CriticalThinking.com

differences. We had previously found that it was not enough to simply ask "How were they similar and how were they different?" when we compare and contrast. To attain greater insight through this kind of thinking, we needed to do more. In this case, we similarly needed to think more deeply and carefully about how these two sources depicted one of the most famous events in American history. By using a thinking strategy map such as the one in Figure 15.1 to make their comparing and contrasting more skillful, students were able not only to focus their thinking but also to probe more deeply into the similarities and differences they identified. You will notice that three additional questions besides "How are they similar?" and "How are they different?" appear on this thinking map. These guided the students to also think about which similarities and differences are important, what patterns can be found in the similarities and differences, and what significant conclusions they can draw from the important similarities and differences. It is the addition of these three questions that leads to more skillful comparing and contrasting than just asking the first two questions.

Using the information from the book and the movie and questions prompted by the thinking strategy map, students then recorded their ideas by completing the graphic organizer shown in Figure 15.2 (based on

FIGURE 15.2

Open Compare and Contrast Exercise

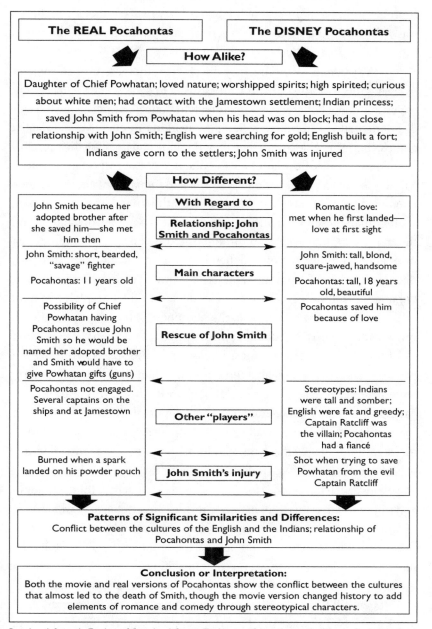

| The REAL Pocahontas | The DISNEY Pocahontas |

How Alike?

Daughter of Chief Powhatan; loved nature; worshipped spirits; high spirited; curious about white men; had contact with the Jamestown settlement; Indian princess; saved John Smith from Powhatan when his head was on block; had a close relationship with John Smith; English were searching for gold; English built a fort; Indians gave corn to the settlers; John Smith was injured

How Different?

The REAL Pocahontas	With Regard to	The DISNEY Pocahontas
John Smith became her adopted brother after she saved him—she met him then	Relationship: John Smith and Pocahontas	Romantic love: met when he first landed—love at first sight
John Smith: short, bearded, "savage" fighter Pocahontas: 11 years old	Main characters	John Smith: tall, blond, square-jawed, handsome Pocahontas: tall, 18 years old, beautiful
Possibility of Chief Powhatan having Pocahontas rescue John Smith so he would be named her adopted brother and Smith would have to give Powhatan gifts (guns)	Rescue of John Smith	Pocahontas saved him because of love
Pocahontas not engaged. Several captains on the ships and at Jamestown	Other "players"	Stereotypes: Indians were tall and somber; English were fat and greedy; Captain Ratcliff was the villain; Pocahontas had a fiancé
Burned when a spark landed on his powder pouch	John Smith's injury	Shot when trying to save Powhatan from the evil Captain Ratcliff

Patterns of Significant Similarities and Differences:
Conflict between the cultures of the English and the Indians; relationship of Pocahontas and John Smith

Conclusion or Interpretation:
Both the movie and real versions of Pocahontas show the conflict between the cultures that almost led to the death of Smith, though the movie version changed history to add elements of romance and comedy through stereotypical characters.

Based on *Infusing the Teaching of Critical and Creative Thinking into Content Instruction: A Lesson Design Handbook for the Elementary Grades* © 1994 The Critical Thinking Co. www.CriticalThinking.com

Swartz & Parks, 1994). However, students also determined that it was equally important to fill in the data accurately by checking their notes from the movie and the text of the book. They realized that a conclusion was only worthy if it was based on accurate information true to the source from which it was extracted.

As the students were guided by this strategy, they also worked cooperatively in groups of three or four while striving to be as precise and accurate as possible about both sources of information. Indeed, by practicing the kind of interdependent thinking fostered by working in effective cooperative groups, they were able to enhance their thinking and increase their insights.

This example illustrates how the practice of two important Habits of Mind — *striving for accuracy and precision* and *thinking interdependently* — enhanced the skillfulness of these students' thinking. Using the thinking strategy map for skillful compare and contrast as a framework and putting the framework into operation through the use of a special graphic organizer allowed students to extend their thinking; at the same time, the practice of these two important Habits of Mind led them to refine and enhance this thinking. The result is reflected in the completed graphic organizer. Now, as we move on to the next phase of the lesson, the graphic organizer also becomes a hard copy of thinking to be used as prewriting.

Prewriting is often the most neglected of the stages of the writing process — and yet it is arguably the most important. It is so much easier to write if students have something "thought-full" to say. It is also so much easier to be accurate if students have a hard copy of their thinking and learning that has itself stressed accuracy. A completed graphic organizer structured to guide a specific type of skillful thinking is not intended as a worksheet. Rather, it is a product of in-depth thinking in which students can change, delete, or add information based on what they think is relevant and important. It is this thinking that provides the substance of what will be communicated in writing when a graphic organizer is treated as a piece of prewriting. The structure of this particular graphic organizer lends itself to the structure of good compare and contrast writing: there is a conclusion that is explicit, as are the similarities and differences that support it. However, students often still have difficulty transferring their thinking to an essay.

Figure 15.3 is what I call a writing map (based on the writing templates found in Swartz, Kiser, & Reagan, 1999). It was developed to help

FIGURE 15.3

Writing Map for Open Compare and Contrast Essay

(To be used with the completed Open Compare and Contrast graphic organizer.)

Audience: _____

Purpose: _____

Paragraph 1—This paragraph is an introduction to your writing.

• **Sentence 1:** Write the conclusion or interpretation from the graphic organizer. It should include the names of the two things that you are comparing and contrasting.

• **Sentence 2:** Write a sentence to elaborate on the first sentence, giving more information about your topic.

• **Sentence 3:** The last sentence should relate to your reader that the two things you are comparing have similarities and differences.

Paragraph 2—This paragraph will explain the similarities that the two things share.
Before you begin this paragraph, you need to choose the three best similarities from your graphic organizer. Number them in order of importance from most important (1) to least important (3).

• **Sentence 1:** This is a topic sentence to tell the reader that the paragraph will contain similarities.

• **Sentences 2 and 3:** State the second most important similarity that you chose. Follow Sentence 2 with an example of how the two things you are comparing meet the similarity.

• **Sentences 4 and 5:** State the least important similarity you chose. Follow Sentence 4 with an elaboration of how the two things you are comparing meet the similarity.

• **Sentences 6 and 7:** State the most important similarity. Follow Sentence 6 with an elaboration of how the two things share this commonality.

Paragraph 3—This paragraph will discuss the differences between the two things.
Choose the three most important categories (listed under the With Regard To box) and number them from most important (1) to least important (3).

• **Sentence 1:** This is a transition sentence between the two paragraphs. It should connect the last sentences of Paragraph 2 to the topic of Paragraph 3. For example, "*Although* _____ *and* _____ *have similarities, they also have differences.*"

(continued)

FIGURE 15.3   *(continued)*

Writing Map for Open Compare and Contrast Essay

- **Sentences 2 and 3:** Write a sentence using the second most important category. Follow Sentence 2 with an example of how each of the two is different in this regard. (You may also write additional sentences giving specific examples.)

- **Sentences 4 and 5:** Write a sentence using the third most important category. Follow Sentence 4 with an example of how each of the two is different in this regard. (You may also write additional sentences giving specific examples.)

- **Sentences 6 and 7:** Write a sentence using the most important category. Then tell the reader how each is different in this regard. (You may also write additional sentences giving specific examples.)

Paragraph 4—This is your concluding paragraph.

- **Sentences 1, 2, and 3:** This is your opportunity to impress the reader with your conclusion. However, it should be worded differently from the first paragraph. The last sentence, the clincher, is what the reader will remember the most.

Hint: Reread your entire essay. Then answer the question "So what?" in your mind. This will help to generate a closing statement.

Based on *Teaching Critical and Creative Thinking and Language Arts: Infusion Lessons Grades 5 and 6* © 1999 The Critical Thinking Co. www.CriticalThinking.com

students organize their writing based on the structure of the thinking in which they had been engaged—in this case, skillful comparing and contrasting. To understand the function of the writing map, think about a road map that is intended to guide the driver over unfamiliar territory. When the route is learned or a new route is desired, the present map is no longer needed or can be adapted to the new route. The purpose of the writing map is much the same in that it serves as a guide to the students to help them to transfer their thinking into an organized composition. A writing map also provides answers to frequently asked questions about the structure of the particular kind of writing required when the teacher is not available. It is important to note that the essays that result are all different as to *what* the students write. The map merely helps them to determine the *how*.

As students experience the writing process, striving for accuracy and precision in both their content and their product, they must consider their audience and the purpose for which they are composing. Providing a place on the map to record these two elements helps the students focus on why and to whom they are writing. Audience and purpose are reflected in the degree of formality used in the writing. For example, an expository composition written to an adult differs greatly in language and format from a friendly letter to a friend.

After the first draft, students exchanged compositions and read them for content, using the graphic organizer and writing map as their guides. The reader then asked the writer questions related to clarity and elaboration. Revisions were then made. Because we were striving for accuracy not only in content but also in form, students then exchanged papers again and looked for grammatical, spelling, and punctuation errors as well as incomplete or confusing sentences.

The following is an example of a checklist that was developed to aid students in checking for accuracy in compositions:

Striving for Accuracy in Compositions

- Be specific about the subject about which you are writing.
- Use precise language and sentence structure appropriate to the audience and purpose.
- Use content vocabulary for specificity.
- Go back to the text or source material and verify that what you are writing is accurate.
- Use what is written on the graphic organizer as a reference.

Another opportunity to revise was given—after all, we are modeling the importance of taking pride in the finished product. Because my school had a computer lab that was available to all, students typed their compositions and made corrections on the computer. Figure 15.4 shows the product of cognitive composition as it relates to the lesson on Pocahontas and is extended to include a piece of compare/contrast writing. It was done by a 5th grade student. The audience was a teacher or parent. The purpose was not only to inform the audience about the similarities and differences of the two versions, but also to reveal the writer's deeper and more careful thinking.

Note that the composition reflects not only skillful thinking related to the content, but also awareness of the writing process. Yes, this required

FIGURE 15.4

5th Grader's Compare/Contrast Essay

Pocahontas: Fact vs. Fiction

The story of Pocahontas has been told in various ways for hundreds of years. In 1607 the English came to the New World to find gold, but instead they discovered "savages." While both *Pocahontas*, the Disney movie and the factual account researched and written by Jean Fritz in *The Double Life of Pocahontas* show an actual historical event that was a result of the conflict between the cultures, they also show the differences between history and Hollywood.

There are some similarities between the movie and actual historical fact. One very important commonality is that both versions have the same main characters: Pocahontas, John Smith, and Powhatan. All three of these people play an important role in both fact and fiction. Powhatan was the chief of the Indian tribe and was Pocahontas's father. This means that he was in control of his people. Pocahontas was a princess who was a free-spirited girl that roamed through the woods. She also lived in both worlds—that of the white and Indian. John Smith, an English captain, was an outsider from England, who was very pleased with the New World in both reality and fiction. He was a bold adventurer who viewed the Indians as savages because they did not dress or act like Englishmen. Another thing they have in common is that both versions had conflict between the cultures of the English and Indians. The Indians dressed, acted, thought, and played differently from the white men. They had different values and a way of living that the English did not understand. A third similarity is probably the one that is best remembered by everyone. Pocahontas saved John Smith from being killed by Powhatan, her father. This event changed the course of history because of the relationship between the Indian princess and the English captain.

Even though there are some similarities in both versions of Pocahontas, there are also quite a few important differences. One difference was the actual relationship between John Smith and Pocahontas. In the movie they met almost as soon as the English landed and they became romantically involved since Pocahontas was shown as a beautiful young woman and John Smith was a handsome Englishman. In reality, the evidence shows that they did not meet until Pocahontas "saved" his life and he became her "adopted" brother. She was really an 11 year old girl and he was a short, bearded man in his late 20's. Another way the movie was different from the actual history was the addition of stereotypes. In the Disney production the Indians were all tall, fierce, and serious. The English were greedy and not very intelligent—except, of course, for John Smith. They were either short and fat or tall and skinny—except again for John Smith, who was tall, blond, and handsome. In real life, there were good guys and bad guys on both sides. Not all of the English were greedy and not all of the Indians were noble. A third way in which they were different was the reason that Pocahontas saved John Smith from being clubbed to death by her father. The actual facts are more interesting than the Hollywood version.

FIGURE 15.4   *(continued)*
5th Grader's Compare/Contrast Essay

Pocahontas actually did throw herself over him and begged for his life. However, in the movie she did it because she loved him. In real life, she had not met him until she asked that he be saved. More precisely, anytime a girl or woman in that particular tribe saved the life of a male captive, he became the adopted son of her father and had to present him with gifts. Since Powhatan wanted guns, it seems likely that her father planned the whole thing!

   The lives of Pocahontas and John Smith were truly exciting ones. If she had not "saved" him, the English would have had a more difficult time in the New World. However, the movie makers did not trust history to be as interesting as their own imagination. They changed fact to fiction to include romance and stereotypical characters and left accuracy for historians. However, no matter the version, the Indian Princess Pocahontas and Captain John Smith will live forever in our history.

several class periods and also time at home as homework. However, the first time a type of writing is introduced, it should be given time, effort, and attention. These three factors show the value a teacher assigns to learning a task or a concept.

   There is one more step in the cognitive composition process that is often overlooked in our rush to get on to another curriculum requirement. Let's review what has taken place so far. Students have learned the historical content of the lesson, differentiated fact from fiction, learned how to extend comparing and contrasting beyond merely listing similarities and differences so that it can be done with skill, thought in depth about what they were going to write before they wrote it, used a writing map to help them organize their compositions, created a checklist for striving for accuracy when writing, and produced a quality product they could be proud of. There was one more thing to do: discuss as a class the elements of cognitive composition that they had just experienced. The following questions are examples of the types of questions that can help to guide this discussion:

   • Was the strategy for skillful comparing and contrasting useful in composing your writing? If so, how? If not, what would you add or remove that will make it more useful?

- How did the use of the graphic organizer affect your ability to know what you wanted to write? Did it affect your ability in any other way? If so, how?
- Did the writing map help you to organize your writing? If so, how? If not, why?
- Would you change the writing map? If so, how?
- What impact, if any, does keeping in mind striving for accuracy have on your writing? What specific things did you do to strive for accuracy?
- Was working together with other students helpful? How? Would you do it again? When? Why?
- In what ways did the thinking that we did beforehand and the thinking you did as you wrote help you develop your final product?
- How will you compose a piece of compare/contrast writing the next time you are asked to write such an essay?

Students may want to start a notebook where they keep copies of thinking maps, graphic organizers, writing maps, final copies, and notes on their responses to the preceding questions for future reference.

I share with my colleagues the idea that teaching students to become skillful thinkers not only involves teaching them important thinking procedures like the one for skillful compare and contrast, and such Habits of Mind as thinking interdependently; it also involves teaching them how they can take charge of their own thinking so that when they face thinking challenges, they can evaluate them and respond with the appropriate type of skillful thinking. This concluding metacognitive activity paves the way for the third important component in thinking-based learning.

Parts-to-Whole Relationships

Everything has parts. Even parts have parts. Keeping that in mind, one of the elements of the curriculum that is difficult for students is reading and interpreting historical documents. It is even harder for them to write about the function of the components of these documents. The following lesson, like the previous one, may be taught in either a social studies or a language arts class. It focuses on the Constitution of the United States as content, teaching students how to skillfully determine parts-to-whole relationships as the thinking objective. In this case, emphasizing the use of clear and precise language as a Habit of Mind enhances achieving this objective.

Like many other teachers, I found the traditional way of teaching students about the Constitution was extremely boring, especially to my students who usually came away from such instruction with little real understanding of this document. Reading, discussing, and answering written questions was a chore with little carryover after the usual test. Students still didn't understand how this document affected their daily lives. The resulting essays were shallow and lackluster. The challenge was to create a lesson on the Constitution that used the elements of cognitive composition.

To skillfully think about the Constitution, we had to become familiar with it first—a daunting task. The Preamble to the Constitution was the key. Because a preamble's purpose is to signal the reader as to the content of what is to come, we asked this question: "Does the Constitution itself fulfill the promises made in the Preamble?" Just to refresh your memory, the Preamble reads as follows:

> We the people of the United States in order to form a more perfect union, establish justice, ensure domestic tranquility, provide for the common defense, promote the general welfare, and secure the blessings of liberty to ourselves and our posterity, do ordain and establish this Constitution for the United States of America.

To clarify our understanding of the language contained in the Preamble and to better answer the question, we used dictionaries to determine the nuances of meaning of those words involved in the promises. The students even decided that they needed to memorize it so that they could think about it more readily. Now, how to make the entire Constitution digestible?

To fully understand a whole it is important to understand the function of its parts. Traditionally when identifying the parts of an object or a process, students would simply assign a label. This would result in a list that looks something like this when applied to the U.S. Constitution:

The Constitution and Its Parts

Preamble
Article I: The Legislative Branch
Article II: The Executive Branch
Article III: The Judicial Branch
Article IV: Relations Between the States
Article V: Amendment Process
Article VI: Supremacy of Federal Law/Addition of New States
Article VII: Guidelines for Ratification

Merely labeling the parts of the Constitution, however, would not result in a deep understanding of the basic law of the United States. To accomplish understanding, a thinking strategy map is needed to guide our thinking about parts-to-whole relationships beyond merely asking and answering the traditional question, "What are the parts of this object?" Asking only this first question ("What smaller parts make up the whole?") would result in a list like the one above. By adding questions that require careful thinking about what would happen to the whole object if a part were missing, what the function of the part is, and how the parts all work together to make the whole operate, a much deeper understanding is attained. The result is a thinking strategy map that represents a basic procedure for skillful parts-to-whole thinking, much like the one in Figure 15.5.

Using this thinking strategy map as our guide, our first task was to identify the parts of the Constitution that followed the Preamble. As listed in the prior example, there are seven main parts, or articles, that designate the responsibilities of the federal government, its branches, and those of the states. Answering Questions 2 and 3 on the map, however, requires more than just remembering the names of these articles. To accomplish this, the class divided into seven teams of three or four members. This was done at random by simply having the students stand in line and numbering them from one through seven. The ones took Article I; the twos, Article II; and so on. Their task was to read the article, determine what would happen to the United States or their daily lives if it were missing, and conversely state in positive terms what the function was. They then presented this information to the class, using clear and precise language (in other words, language specifically related to the content). Each group recorded their findings on a graphic organizer designed for these purposes

FIGURE 15.5

Thinking Strategy Map for Parts-to-Whole Relationships

1. What smaller things make up the whole?

2. For each part, what would happen if it was missing?

3. What is the function of each part?

4. How do the parts work together to make the whole what it is or operate as it does?

From *Infusing the Teaching of Critical and Creative Thinking into Content Instruction: A Lesson Design Handbook for the Elementary Grades* © 1994 The Critical Thinking Co. www.CriticalThinking.com

(based on Swartz & Parks, 1994). Figure 15.6 is the graphic organizer for Article V, which deals with amending the Constitution.

When the results of using the thinking strategy map to determine the function of each of the articles had been presented to the whole class, we then completed the top part of the graphic organizer shown in Figure 15.7 (based on Swartz & Parks, 1994). This was our preparation for having each student write a short essay to answer the last question on the thinking strategy map. As in the previous example of comparing and contrasting, this graphic organizer became our prewriting. Notice how the considerable thought that had already gone into what the students wrote on the previous graphic organizer is now included in this summary of the class's work.

Much as they had in the compare/contrast example, students used a writing map as a guide in composing a one-paragraph essay using the class graphic organizer as prewriting. Figure 15.8 shows the writing map.

Because this was the first time we had done this kind of thinking and writing, we again followed the writing process described in the preceding lesson. The purpose was to write an explanation, for a history textbook, of how the parts of the U.S. Constitution work together. Therefore, it would follow that the intended audience was students who would be reading the textbook. The students exchanged papers for revising and editing. However, this time they used the class graphic organizer as a guide to make

FIGURE 15.6
**Parts-to-Whole Graphic Organizer
for Article V of the U.S. Constitution**

DETERMINING PARTS-TO-WHOLE RELATIONSHIPS

THE WHOLE OBJECT

The U.S. Constitution

PARTS OF THE OBJECT

Article I	Article II	Article III	Article IV	Article V	Article VI	Article VII

**PART
CONSIDERED
V**

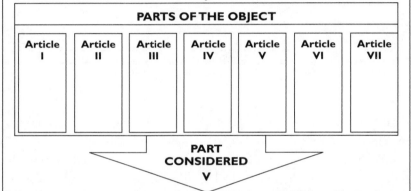

**WHAT WOULD HAPPEN TO THE OBJECT
IF THE PART WERE MISSING?**

Without Article V there would be no way to change the Constitution or to add on to it. We still would be living with laws that were made in the late 1700s. For example, we would still have slavery, and women would not be allowed to vote. The president would have no term limits and could serve for life. The vice president would still be the president's opponent in the election—so how well do you think they would get along?

WHAT IS THE FUNCTION OF THE PART?

Amendment V's function is to provide a process by which the Constitution can be changed or added on to. This process is not a fast one so that people have time to think about what they are doing. By amending the Constitution we can make changes that "fix" what is wrong with the original document—or add on to it if necessary. It allows us to become a more "perfect union."

Based on *Infusing the Teaching of Critical and Creative Thinking into Content Instruction: A Lesson Design Handbook for the Elementary Grades* © 1994 The Critical Thinking Co. www.CriticalThinking.com

FIGURE 15.7

Parts-to-Whole Graphic Organizer for the U.S. Constitution

DETERMINING PARTS-TO-WHOLE RELATIONSHIPS

THE WHOLE OBJECT

The U.S. Constitution

▼

PARTS OF THE OBJECT

Article I	Article II	Article III	Article IV	Article V	Article VI	Article VII
MADE UP OF THESE PARTS	MADE UP OF THESE PARTS	MADE UP OF THESE PARTS	MADE UP OF THESE PARTS	MADE UP OF THESE PARTS	MADE UP OF THESE PARTS	MADE UP OF THESE PARTS
Legislative Branch	Executive Branch	Judicial Branch	Relations Between the States	Amendment Process	Supremacy of Federal Law; Addition of New States	Guidelines for Ratification

WHAT WOULD HAPPEN TO THE OBJECT IF THE PARTS WERE MISSING?

| People not represented—no Congress; the president would be too powerful. | People could break laws since there would be no one to enforce them. Congress could pass any law. No president. | No federal courts or Supreme Court to interpret the laws. People's rights not protected. | Each state would be its own "country." Criminals could cross state lines and not be punished. States unprotected if attacked. | Constitution would have only seven articles—no way to amend it. Women could not vote; would still have slavery; no guaranteed rights. | Laws would change from state to state—federal law under state law. No new states. Going from state to state would be difficult. | Constitution not in effect. States don't have to commit to the union. Each state would be a separate nation. |

WHAT IS THE FUNCTION OF THE PARTS?

| To provide a process for making laws, giving people representation, etc. Legislative branch to check and balance power. | To provide a means by which the laws are enforced and provide the method to elect a president and vice president. To check and balance the power of Congress. | To protect the Constitution and the rights of the people. Establish the judicial branch to check the power of Congress and the president. Supreme Court. | To make the laws consistent across the states and to provide the method by which new states could be added. | Allows the Constitution to grow and change by providing the process by which it could be amended. | Requires that federal law be supreme to state law. Makes sure that federal officials must promise to uphold the Constitution. | Provides for the process for ratification, which made each state commit in writing to the new government. |

WHAT IS THE RELATIONSHIP BETWEEN THE PARTS AND THE WHOLE?

The Articles all work together to form the basic law of our country—the Constitution. It integrates us together as a whole, as one people. They function much like the parts of a bicycle. The handlebars provide the balance, like the branches of government established by Articles I, II, and III balance power. The states are the spokes that are held together by the hub of the Constitution in Articles IV and VI. All kinds of accessories can be added on as well as changed, which is what Article V does. In order for the bicycle to function, it must have a rider. This is like Article VII, which required the states to join in order for the nation to be formed. All of the parts of the Constitution were put in motion by the people, who strive to be a more perfect union.

Based on *Infusing the Teaching of Critical and Creative Thinking into Content Instruction: A Lesson Design Handbook for the Elementary Grades* © 1994 The Critical Thinking Co. www.CriticalThinking.com

FIGURE 15.8

Writing Map for Parts-to-Whole One-Paragraph Essay

(To be used with the completed graphic organizers for Parts-to-Whole Relationships.)

Audience: _____

Purpose: _____

Sentence 1: Name the whole object and tell something about it.

Sentence 2: Extend or elaborate the ideas in Sentence 1.

Sentence 3 to Conclusion: Discuss *each* of the parts and tell how its function contributes to the overall operation of the whole or the way it serves its purpose. This will take several sentences. Make sure you use the graphic organizer to check off each part as you write about it.

Conclusion: This sentence is the most powerful part of your essay. It should not only include the name of the whole, but also be a memorable statement that will leave your reader impressed by your skillful thinking!

---

sure that the paper they were reading had all the required parts. Keep in mind that we practiced cognitive composition, which involves explicit use of skillful thinking—an element of which is the Habit of Mind we were practicing. The result was a checklist like this:

Using Clear and Precise Language in Composition

- Use what is written on the graphic organizer as a reference.
- Use the specific vocabulary of the content.
- Use clarifying sentences to explain what your audience may not understand or know.
- Use language that is appropriate to the audience and purpose.
- Use a dictionary to look up words with "fuzzy" meanings.

Because students had just completed a series of lessons on similes and metaphors, many wished to incorporate that learning into their writing. Figure 15.9 is a final composition written by a 5th grader.

Not only were the students surprised by how much they had learned about the basic law of the nation and its effect on their lives; so were the parents! Again, we completed our cognitive composition by discussing

FIGURE 15.9
Student Essay on the U.S. Constitution

The Constitution

The Articles all work together to form the basic law of our country—the Constitution. It integrates us together as a whole, as one people. These Articles function much like the parts of a bicycle. The handlebars provide the balance a rider needs to move forward much like the branches of government established by Articles I, II, and III balance power between the president, Congress, and courts. This allows us to move forward as a country since it establishes justice, provides for the common defense, promotes the general welfare, and secures the blessings of liberty for all of the people who live here. The states are the spokes that are held together by the hub of the Constitution in Articles IV and VI in order to secure domestic tranquility. Sometimes a bicycle doesn't have all it needs to work as well as it could. Just like the government sometimes needs new laws to make it function better. New accessories can be added or changes made because of Article V which allows for amending the Constitution. In order for a bicycle to function, it must have a rider. Article VII provided for this when it required the states to join in order for the nation to be formed. All the parts of the Constitution were put in motion by the people—striving to be a more perfect union.

Based on *Infusing the Teaching of Critical and Creative Thinking into Content Instruction: A Lesson Design Handbook for the Elementary Grades* © 1994 The Critical Thinking Co. www.CriticalThinking.com

our engagement with the process and determining if there was anything we would change, delete, or add. Here are some prompting questions we used:

• Was the strategy for skillful parts-to-whole relationships useful in your writing? If so, how? If not, what would you add or remove that will make it more useful?

• How did the use of the graphic organizer affect your ability to know what you wanted to write? Did it affect your writing in other ways?

• What role did the writing map play in the development of your writing?

• Would you change the writing map? If so, how?

• What impact, if any, did keeping in mind the need to use clear and precise language have on your writing? What specific things did you do and think about to make sure that your language was clear and precise?

• Was working together with other students helpful in your writing? How? Would you do this again? When? Why?

• In what ways did the thinking you did beforehand and the thinking you did as you wrote help you to develop your final product?

• How will you do this the next time you are asked to write about parts-to-whole relationships?

As an extension, the class decided to explore metaphors for the Constitution. After determining if a proposed metaphor contain similarities between the item and the object and if there were any differences, the students wrote a modified diamonte. Clear and precise language is even more important in poetry—especially when using such a structured form. The limits that are placed on the number and function of words require that students thoroughly explore exactly what they want to say and how they are going to say it. Here is a standard form for a diamonte:

Noun

Adjective, Adjective

Ing word, Ing word, Ing word

Noun, Noun, Noun, Noun

Ing word, Ing word, Ing word

Adjective, Adjective

Noun

The first three and a half lines are about the top noun, and the last three and a half lines concern the last noun. The students modified the form by making the diamonte a metaphor in which all lines had to relate to both. Here is an example:

Constitution

Provident, Strong

Supporting, Lasting, Changing

Freedom, Power, Structure, Form

Protecting, Surrounding, Uniting

Intricate, Flexible

Spider Web

Decision Making

The third example of cognitive composition has at its center the fine art of persuasion. In this case a cognitive composition flowed from a skillful-thinking lesson on the Newbery Award–winning novel *Shiloh* by Phyllis Reynolds Naylor (1991). We used skillful decision making as the thinking objective and a writing process that would result in a persuasive letter, all enhanced by an emphasis on the Habit of Mind of understanding and respecting, or empathizing with, other points of view.

The students had read *Shiloh* to the point where a pivotal decision will chart the direction the characters will take for the rest of the book. Here is a brief synopsis of what has occurred so far: Marty Preston is a member of a poor family in Friendly, West Virginia. His father, a rural postman, has refused to let him have a dog because it would be one more mouth to feed. When a young beagle follows Marty home from Shiloh Bridge one day, his father insists he return the dog to its owner, Judd Travers. Mr. Travers, however, is known to abuse animals, and, sure enough, when the dog is returned to him, he threatens to break its legs if it runs away again. But the dog *does* run away again and returns to Marty. It is then that Marty names the beagle Shiloh. Knowing what will happen to Shiloh if he takes the dog back to Judd, Marty hides it in the woods. After a while, Mrs. Preston becomes suspicious and follows Marty to Shiloh's hiding place.

This is the situation that makes a decision necessary for Mrs. Preston. What should she do? Figure 15.10 shows the thinking strategy map for skillful decision making that helped to guide us through the lesson.

As we worked our way through this thinking strategy map, the students found many options for Mrs. Preston—which brings up an important point. It is critical in teaching this skill that the second question not limit choices. If we had asked, "Should Mrs. Preston keep the secret or not?" then the options would have been limited to two, and the important step of brainstorming various options to explore would have been lost. This brainstorming is key to the subsequent writing and to the emphasis on empathy.

I would be remiss at this point if I did not explain activities from the beginning of the school year, when this class spent a great deal of time

FIGURE 15.10
Thinking Strategy Map for Skillful Decision Making

---

1. What makes a decision necessary?

2. What are my options?

3. What are the likely consequences of each option?

4. How important are the consequences?

5. Which option is best in light of the consequences?

From *Infusing the Teaching of Critical and Creative Thinking into Content Instruction: A Lesson Design Handbook for the Elementary Grades* © 1994 The Critical Thinking Co. www.CriticalThinking.com

laying the groundwork for empathizing with and understanding others' motives and actions. We filled boards and charts with all the things we could think of that influenced ourselves and others. As we wrote them down, we discussed the *how* and *why* of the influence. We typed the result on the class computer, ran it off, and put it in our notebooks. As we thought of other examples throughout the year, we added them to our list—but only after we had discussed the item in class. Parents often offered suggestions at home or when they came to school. Many were predictable: race, height, weight, religion, climate, economic background, and handicaps, for example. Some were not usual: traumatic events such as living through a tornado or a hurricane, addictions, abuse, and classroom environment. Using the list, the students were asked to choose a different point of view, to look at it in depth, and to write either poetry or prose that would reflect "walking in that person's moccasins." The results were extraordinary. Figure 15.11 presents an example written by a 5th grader (Reagan, 2001).

Empathy for, and understanding of, other people's motives and actions is essential when reading novels and using the information that has been gathered to write either poetry or prose. One student said that "you have to listen with your mind as you read so that when you write you can reach your audience's thoughts with your words." That's profound thinking for a 10-year-old.

FIGURE 15.11

A 5th Grader's Empathy Poem

Blindness

My appearance is fairly normal.
On the outside I look the same.
There's something you may not notice,
And it sometimes causes me sadness and pain.
There are people who make fun of me,
And there are some that understand
That my life is kind of different
Because I don't see things like they can.
The pictures in my mind are different.
They are like those in an antique book.
The shades I see are mainly black and white
Like the photos your great-grandparents took.
I may not see the colors
In a rainbow like you do.
My senses help me see them
In a way that's unique from you.
Red is not a color.
To me it's the feeling of love.
Yellow is the warmth of the sun on my face,
And blue is the air above.
Green is the smell of newly cut grass,
And white is the softness of snow.
I wish I could see colors like you do,
But that's a world I will never know.

From Lacy Burress, used with permission.

As we approached the best way to tackle the many options that the students had brainstormed for Mrs. Preston, the class decided to work in groups of three or four—each choosing an option that they thought was worth considering (though they were prepared to reject it if, based on the results of Question 4, it turned out not to be viable). Some groups worked on the same option but went about exploring it differently. Using what they had previously learned about understanding and empathizing with others, they became Mrs. Preston. They considered the consequences of the option they chose, both positive and negative, and, for each of these, any evidence from the text that would prove that the consequence was or was not likely to occur (assuming that we needed to weigh more heavily those consequences that were likely). Then they assigned a value to the consequence based on how important it was from Mrs. Preston's point of view. Taking all the data into consideration, they decided if the option was a good one for Mrs. Preston.

Note how through this entire process, these 10- and 11-year-olds had to think about the situation from Mrs. Preston's point of view—that of an adult and a mother. They had to listen with their minds and watch her actions, starting from all the events leading up to this one to help them determine what the influences were in her life. They had to think about the day-to-day elements of her life and how this decision would affect them. The ability to "become" an adult had been honed by the lessons we had engaged in at the beginning of the year. Figure 15.12 is an example of one of the many graphic organizers, each a little different from the others, that resulted (Swartz et al., 1999).

The notations on the graphic organizer (plus and minus signs, and checkmarks) refer back to the thinking strategy map for skillful decision making. Question 3 asks "What are the likely consequences of each option?" Students first determine if it is a positive (+) or negative (–) consequence. Then they find and record evidence from the text that shows that the consequence will or will not occur, which in turn results in a checkmark for those that are likely and a line through those that are not. The right-hand column contains the answer, for each likely consequence, to Question 4, which deals with the value or importance of the consequence. The rating scale was a simple one: Very Important, Important, and Not Very Important. Based on all of this information, the students then determined if the option was a good one. The groups then presented their findings to the whole class—which inspired a lively discussion about each option's merits, sometimes involving serious disagreements between students.

This decision-making activity concluded with each student comparing the various results and then answering the last question on the thinking strategy map: "Which option is best?" Each group was given copies of the other groups' completed graphic organizers so they would be able to compare all the options considered.

FIGURE 15.12

Example of a Graphic Organizer for Skillful Decision Making

OPTIONS	
What can <u>Marty's mother</u> do?	
• Go down the hill and tell Marty's father now. • Keep Marty's secret from his father. • Tell Marty's father about Shiloh later. • Tell Marty that he must tell his father himself. • Take Shiloh to the house. • Call the animal shelter to take Shiloh away. • Find another place for Shiloh to hide.	• Pretend she saw nothing. • Call Judd to come pick up his dog. • Take Shiloh to Judd herself. • Take Shiloh to the vet. • Teach Marty a lesson by turning him in to the police for stealing. Call a lawyer. • Try to convince her husband to keep the secret. • Make Marty take Shiloh back to Judd and not tell Pa.

Option Considered:
Keep Marty's secret
and tell no one.

CONSEQUENCES	VALUE
What will happen if <u>Marty's mother</u> takes this option?	How important is the consequence? Why?
− Pa finds out and never trusts his wife again. ✓	**Very important:** Trust between a husband and wife is the foundation of a strong family. Everyone would feel the effect.
− Ma feels so guilty about lying to her husband that she becomes mentally ill. ✓	**Important:** Ma would feel guilty, but she is a strong woman and has a strong faith.
+ Shiloh stays hidden and safe.	
− Pa discovers Shiloh himself, con- + fronts Ma, and forgives her. ✓	**Very Important:** Understanding and forgiving are part of a strong family. It would set a good example for the children.
− Marty's father finds out and leaves the family. ✓	
+ Marty's mother cannot stand keeping anything from her husband and confesses. ✓	**Very important:** Ma would no longer have to live with keeping a secret from her husband.

From *Teaching Critical and Creative Thinking in Language Arts: Infusion Lessons Grades 5 and 6* © 1999 The Critical Thinking Co. www.CriticalThinking.com

When they engaged in this process, the students were told that they should be prepared to defend their choices. This, in turn, prepared them for the final phase of this lesson — writing a persuasive letter to Mrs. Preston recommending an option and explaining why it was the best one. The students were asked to write about what they considered the top three options and to use the writing map shown in Figure 15.13 (Swartz, Kiser, & Reagan, 1999).

As with the previous lessons, the students helped each other revise and edit their compositions. One of the rules in the class was, as the year progressed, students could not work on the same editing teams. This created diversity in the teams and encouraged students to work with people outside their immediate group of friends. Again, they could only ask questions related to clarity and elaboration, keeping hurt feelings to a minimum. An example of a final composition appears in Figure 15.14 (Swartz, Kiser, & Reagan, 1999).

We were, of course, not finished yet. We again discussed the elements of cognitive composition and how they worked separately and together to form the whole. How did the Habit of Mind of listening with empathy and understanding influence us as writers and as interdependent, independent thinkers? How would we change the writing map to make it more useful? What else could we do to be more empathetic and understanding of others? This, of course, is an important question, not just for a 5th grade language arts class, but for life.

Skillful thinking as defined in *Thinking-Based Learning* (Swartz et al., 2007) is "a self-planned, proficient, and purposeful application of appropriate thinking skills without skipping any key operations, using relevant skill-related knowledge and supported by appropriate important mental habits" (p. 1). It is instructional contexts like those described in this chapter — which emphasize and help students practice important habits of mind, such as those identified in the work of Art Costa and Bena Kallick — that have the most instructional force and contribute most to the development of our students as good thinkers, good readers, and good writers. The keys for effective writing are found in these elements of skillful thinking infused into instruction that emphasizes the writing process. The implementation of cognitive composition in the classroom creates an environment in which

FIGURE 15.13
Writing Map for Decision Making—
Recommending the Best Option

Persuasive Letter

(To be used after completing at least three Skillful Decision Making graphic organizers.)

This persuasive letter will be used to convince your reader to take an action that you recommend. You will use at least three completed decision making graphic organizers that have each explored a different option. Before you begin writing, rank the options from strongest (1) to weakest (3).

Audience: _____

Purpose: _____

Paragraph 1—This paragraph is your opportunity to gain the attention of the person to whom you are writing.
• Explain the situation that makes the decision necessary.
• State the purpose of the letter.
• List the options that you are going to discuss.

Paragraph 2—This paragraph is to inform your reader about the option you ranked second strongest (2).
State the second strongest of the options and discuss it with regard to its positive and negative consequences. Support each consequence with evidence and explain its importance. (Total of 8–10 sentences)

Paragraph 3—This paragraph is to inform your reader about the option you ranked the weakest (3).
State the weakest of the options and discuss it with regard to its positive and negative consequences. Support each consequence with evidence and explain its importance. (Total of 8–10 sentences)

Paragraph 4—This paragraph is to inform your reader about the option you ranked the strongest (1).
State the strongest of the options (the one you think is best) and discuss it with regard to its positive and negative consequences. Support each consequence with evidence and explain its importance. (Total of 8–10 sentences)

Paragraph 5—This paragraph is your last chance to convince the person to whom you are writing that the option you are recommending is the best one.
Make your recommendation again. Give the strongest reasons why it is the best one. Close your letter with something like this: *Thank you for your consideration* or *Please consider my recommendation.* (Total of 4–5 sentences)

From *Teaching Critical and Creative Thinking in Language Arts: Infusion Lessons Grades 5 and 6* © 1999 The Critical Thinking Co. www.CriticalThinking.com

FIGURE 15.14

**Example of a Student Composition Related
to Skillful Decision Making**

Dear Mrs. Preston,

    You have discovered Marty's secret. He is keeping the dog Shiloh from Judd because he fears that Judd will kill it. You are faced with a tough choice. The purpose of this letter is to recommend what I think you should do. It may seem to you that you have to decide whether to tell Marty's father or not. However, there are many options other than just those two. You could keep Marty's secret and tell no one, make Marty take Shiloh back to Judd and not tell your husband, or take Shiloh back to the house and show him to Marty's father.

    If you make Marty take Shiloh back to Judd and not tell pa that you found him, there are several negative consequences and not too many positive ones. Most likely your husband would find out. After all he is a postman and they visit with everyone. He feels very strongly about the fact that Shiloh belongs to Judd and he would be embarrassed in front of Judd. Being so mean and cruel, Judd might have Marty arrested, although he often breaks the law by killing deer out of season. Judd might even kill Shiloh. He has a history of abusing his dogs and has threatened to break Shiloh's legs if he found him.

    Another option you might consider is to keep Marty's secret and tell no one. It is obvious that you believe that telling the truth is extremely important. It is part of your deep faith in God. When you made Marty tell the truth about eating Dara Lynn's treat, you showed how you felt about lying. Omission is another form of lying. You might even feel so guilty that it would change your relationship with your husband and family. Pa also might find out since he often goes hunting. He would probably be mad at you at first, but you seem to have a strong marriage so he most likely will forgive you. However, there would be some pretty miserable moments first. Guilt is hard to live with.

    Probably the best option of the three is to take Shiloh back to the house, show it to Marty's father and explain the situation to him as best you can. You have a very good relationship with your husband and he listens to you. Even though he feels strongly about property, he might help to think of another solution besides giving the dog back to Judd. Because you have told the truth, you would not feel guilty, and Marty would see that the truth is very important because you were a good role model. Although Shiloh might have to go back to Judd, Marty's father might be more understanding about the situation and he might tell Judd that he is going to be watching to see if he hurts Shiloh.

    If you look at these three options, each has both positive and negative consequences. Because you value the truth so highly and more good things can come out of taking Shiloh back to the house and talking to Marty's father, that is the option that I recommend to you. It will keep the trusting relationship that you have with your husband and show Marty that truth is of great value. Thank you for your consideration and attention. Please think carefully before you make a decision. The future of your family could depend on it.

Sincerely,

From *Teaching Critical and Creative Thinking in Language Arts: Infusion Lessons Grades 5 and 6* © 1999 The Critical Thinking Co. www.CriticalThinking.com

the blank page will no longer be frightening, but rather will be something to fill with exciting and intelligent ideas that are the product of skillful thinking and are expressed in informative, compelling, and powerful writing. The keys work, the door is open . . . I invite you to walk through.

References

The American heritage dictionary of the English language (4th ed.). (2000). Boston: Houghton Mifflin.

Dictionary.com Unabridged. Based on the Random House Unabridged Dictionary. (2006). Available: http://dictionary.reference.com/help/luna.html

Fritz, J. (1987). *The double life of Pocahontas.* New York: Puffin Books.

Naylor, P. R. (1991). *Shiloh.* New York: Macmillan.

Reagan, R. (2001). Developing a lifetime of literacy. In A. Costa (Ed.), *Developing minds: A resource book for teaching thinking* (3rd ed., pp. 337–342). Alexandria, VA: ASCD.

Swartz, R., Costa, A., Beyer, B., Reagan, R., & Kallick, B. (2007). *Thinking-based learning: Activating students' potential.* Norwood, MA: Christopher-Gordon.

Swartz, B., Kiser, M., & Reagan, R. (1999). *Teaching critical and creative thinking in language arts: Infusion lessons grades 5 and 6.* Pacific Grove, CA: Critical Thinking Books and Software.

Swartz, R., & Parks, S. (1994). *Infusing the teaching of critical and creative thinking into content instruction: A lesson design handbook for the elementary grades.* Pacific Grove, CA: Critical Thinking Books and Software.

16

Habits of Mind
and Mathematical Processes

Kevin Clune

After successfully using the Habits of Mind in my 7th grade mathematics classroom for the first time in 2006–2007, I decided to use them again the following school year. A new, additional 20-minute mentoring period with my students allowed me to plan for more expansive use of the habits.

I find that the habits are useful in furthering my objectives of promoting students' development of higher-order thinking skills, their development as self-directed, autonomous learners, and their mastery of academic content. The Habits of Mind provide a framework that helps my students understand these learning objectives and guides them in their development, and a common classroom vernacular that facilitates communication with my students on academic and management issues.

I became interested in the Habits of Mind as a framework for the learning activities that are directed toward the process standards in New York State's mathematics curriculum. The learning standards promulgated by New York State include five process strands: Problem Solving, Reasoning and Proof, Communication, Connections, and Representation. While developing a curriculum for my mathematics classes, I have been trying to find a way to make the learning experiences for these process strands more precise, directed, and cohesive—particularly for the Problem Solving and Reasoning and Proof strands. As I became familiar with the Habits of Mind, I realized that the thought processes they seek to develop are synonymous with the thought processes I want to help my students understand and develop. I believe that, for most students, the long-term relevancy and importance of math comes more from the development of their mental processes than from the mastery of the content. The habits provide an engaging concept to guide the learning experiences that are intended to develop these mental processes. I use the habits as my framework for instruction in process. The framework begins with the first unit of the year. I start the school year with an introduction to the Habits of Mind and several lessons that are directed toward developing an understanding of them.

Introduction to the Habits of Mind

When I introduce the Habits of Mind to my students, I use the following essential question as the starting point: What are the Habits of Mind and how can they help us to think as math problem solvers?

I use the lessons described in the following sections to introduce the habits. Once we go through these introductory lessons, I expect that students will apply the habits throughout the school year. As you will see, I consider metacognition to be the most important Habit of Mind. It is the "big picture" habit that all the others work to bring about.

As noted, state standards delineate a host of process standards that should be part of the 8th grade math learning experience. Habits of Mind are used during these introductory lessons as a guide for the process development. I do not present these lessons in sequence; rather they are interspersed among my lessons in the first quarter of the school year as they become relevant to the content under study.

Lesson Descriptions

Lesson 1: Exploring and Discovering Habits of Mind

This lesson focuses on a discussion of the Habits of Mind and self-analysis for seven of the most important habits: (1) Striving for accuracy, (2) Managing impulsivity, (3) Persisting, (4) Thinking about thinking, (5) Listening with understanding and empathy, (6) Taking responsible risks, and (7) Applying past knowledge to new situations. After students read the article to become familiar with the Habits of Mind, I bring the habits to life in the classroom by having groups of students make posters for each one. Each poster consists of a drawing, a logo or symbol; a statement of how the Habit of Mind can be used in math class; and a poem, rap, skit, or slogan. These posters are shared and then kept up in the classroom during the year to reinforce the students' use of the habits. Students are expected to understand and reflect on what the habits are and how they will guide our studies during the school year. They complete the Intellectual Dispositions Checklist and scoring sheet shown in Figure 16.1 to evaluate their relative strengths in the seven habits. They also answer these reflection questions:

- What habits did you use in class while you were solving the puzzles? Try to provide an example of how you used that habit.
- Which three habits are most important? Explain why.
- Which three habits represent your strengths? Explain why.
- Which three habits represent your weaknesses? Explain why.

The assessments for Lesson 1 include the following:

- Authentic work product: Habit of Mind poster
- Individual open-ended, extended response: Habits of Mind reflection homework

Lesson 2: What Did You Learn Last Year?
Applying Past Knowledge to New Situations

Math is a subject that uses the prior year's learning as a foundation for the subsequent year. In this lesson, students work in groups to review what they know and complete a worksheet of review problems to recall their prior algebra content. The topics are (1) the distributive property, (2) combining like terms, and (3) solving equations with variables on both sides. PowerPoint and Web-based applets are provided so that students can engage in a self-directed review. Students evaluate what they know using a practice test as a warm-up. They then work in groups to correct any errors and clarify any misunderstandings about the warm-up quiz problems and to complete a set of practice problems. Later in the unit, students apply their prior knowledge in a new situation as they are introduced to diagram-based geometry problems whose solutions require a synthesis

FIGURE 16.1

Intellectual Dispositions Checklist

Disposition Question	Always	Often	Some-times	Rarely or Never
1. I always check my work and revise.				
2. I stop, think, and take my time before doing a task.				
3. I keep trying in spite of my frustration.				
4. I am aware of how I am thinking when faced with a problem.				
5. I stop to think before I speak or act.				
6. I ask questions when I don't know what to do.				
7. I can control my strong reactions to events and people.				
8. I am sensitive to thoughts and feelings of others.				
9. I like to be out of my comfort zone.				
10. I plan ahead.				
11. I work out problems by thinking them through, step-by-step.				
12. I always try to hold my work to a high standard.				
13. I try to think about what I already know when I am faced with something new.				
14. I like to push my limits in knowledge and abilities.				
15. I am aware of the types of situations in which I learn best.				
16. I like to try new things.				
17. I am able to put myself in someone else's shoes.				
18. I really enjoy the satisfaction of succeeding in a challenging new task.				
19. I take a chance with new ideas when appropriate.				
20. I like to see the big picture of ideas and how everything fits together.				
21. Near enough is not good enough for me.				
22. I see knowledge like a jigsaw puzzle; all the pieces fit together.				
23. I persevere with tasks even when answers or solutions are not immediately apparent.				
24. I enjoy listening to other possibilities and approaches.				
25. I find trying new things very exciting.				
26. I want to know and understand how I tend to learn.				
27. I think about the similarities between past experiences and new experiences.				
28. I constantly strive to improve the quality of my work.				
29. I am prepared to put up with frustration and confusion to achieve my goals.				
30. I try to imagine what others are thinking and feeling.				
31. I rely on my own thinking as a resource for problem solving.				
32. I refuse to quit even when the going gets tough.				
33. I identify my strengths, limitations, and ways I can improve.				
34. I like to seek out other points of view.				
35. I believe careful planning and preparation are important to achieve success.				

(continued)

FIGURE 16.1   *(continued)*

Intellectual Dispositions Checklist

Evaluation Charts

Match the question number on the Checklist (p. 183) with the question number on the Evaluation Chart (below). Score your relative strengths: Always = 4; Often = 3; Sometimes = 2; Rarely or Never = 1

No.	Score
1.	
6.	
12.	
21.	
28.	

Add scores for
Striving for Accuracy = _____

No.	Score
2.	
5.	
7.	
10.	
35.	

Add scores for
Managing Impulsivity = _____

No.	Score
3.	
18.	
23.	
29.	
32.	

Add scores for Persistence = _____

No.	Score
4.	
11.	
15.	
26.	
33.	

Add scores for Metacognition = _____

No.	Score
8.	
17.	
24.	
30.	
34.	

Add scores for Listening with
Understanding and Empathy = _____

No.	Score
9.	
14.	
16.	
19.	
25.	

Add scores for
Taking Responsible Risks = _____

No.	Score
13.	
20.	
22.	
27.	
31.	

Add scores for Apply Past
Knowledge to New Situations = _____

Relative Strengths Chart

Order	Score	Habit
1st		
2nd		
3rd		
4th		
5th		
6th		
7th		

of newly acquired understandings of angle relationships with their earlier acquired algebra skills.

Assessments for Lesson 2 include the following:

- Quiz: Standards-based quiz on algebra content
- Unit test: Comprehensive unit content test for algebra and problem solving, modeling New York State assessment questions for these concepts

Lesson 3: How Do You Solve That Puzzle?
Thinking About Thinking

I view metacognition as the "holy grail" of the Habits of Mind. Because of that central importance, I use a WebQuest lesson designed to initiate a self-analysis of student thinking in a problem-solving exercise. The lesson is intended to introduce the concept of metacognition and to serve as a jumping-off point for several lessons in which the students are applying their math skills to solve problems that are new and unfamiliar to them. The goal is for them to experience the metacognitive process. They first must observe and analyze a phenomenon, and then they must extend their content knowledge to quantify this phenomenon in a mathematical way. In this case, students solve a puzzle called the peg puzzle (see the version at http://nlvm.usu.edu/en/nav/frames_asid_182_g_3_t_1. html) and must be able to explain how they solved it. The puzzle progresses in difficulty as the number of pieces used increases from two to four to six, and so on. We focus on the thought processes that go into solving the puzzle rather than the outcome. We share the methods that the students used to solve the puzzle. The best explanations are those that recognize and incorporate the numerical pattern in the moves needed to solve the problem. The students share and evaluate one another's solutions. This lesson, like all those described here, would typically be labeled "discovery learning," but with the Habits of Mind element, we add an overlay of consciousness about the problem-solving methodology. Our discussion of that process is aided by our common understanding of and ability to relate our experiences in the lessons to the Habits of Mind.

Assessments for Lesson 3 include the following:

- Performance assessment: Puzzle solving for pairs

Lesson 4: Prove It!

The overall goal of this lesson is to have students engage their higher-order processing skills in a critical thinking task. Students observe and quantify a geometric relationship presented in a Java-based applet called "How High?" that is available on the Internet (http://nlvm.usu.edu/en/nav/frames_asid_275_g_3_t_3.html). They derive a valid mathematical formula that can be used to predict the unknown value based upon their observations. The creation of this formula requires students to synthesize their knowledge of geometry (volume), transformation of formulas, and properties of mathematics into an integrated and cohesive body of knowledge as they apply all of these areas of knowledge to the performance of the task. The objective of this lesson is to integrate several mathematical concepts into a unified whole. Through this integration, students experience how mathematical thinking is analogous to and can be adapted to other areas, such as the law. Students explore their own thinking and enhance their ability to express that thought process to others. Students experience a real-world application of the use of mathematics as they analyze and quantify the problem presented in the "How High?" applet.

Assessments for Lesson 4 include the following:

• Authentic work product: Group brief submitted at conclusion of activity

Lesson 5: Linear Equations

This lesson is designed to engage higher-order thinking skills by providing a learning experience that allows students to observe, quantify, and justify their observations and quantifications about graphs of linear equations. Students are introduced to the slope intercept form of a linear equation, $y = mx + b$. Students use a Web-based activity called "Slope Slider" (http://www.shodor.org/interactivate/activities/SlopeSlider/) to observe the changes that occur in the graphs of linear equations when the slope and y-intercept are manipulated by the user. Students analyze and evaluate the changes that adjusting the slope slider and intercept slider cause to the graph and equation to uncover that m is the slope of the line and that b is the y-intercept. Students use this understanding to advance their mathematical skill set by adding the skills of graphing lines directly from equations and finding equations directly from graphs of lines. Students use their understanding to graph a line given the slope and a point. Students justify their observations and quantifications by connecting to and corroborating their findings by finding ordered pairs that are solutions to the equation algebraically and graphically.

Assessments for Lesson 5 include the following:

• Ticket-to-exit quiz: Standards-based quiz on linear equations content

• Unit test: Comprehensive unit test for linear equations and problem solving, modeling New York State assessment questions for these concepts

Lesson 6: Venn Do You Use This?
Selecting a Strategy for Problem Solving

For this lesson I combine two topics, logic problems and Venn diagrams, and initiate a discovery learning WebQuest exercise for the Venn diagrams, using a compare-and-contrast approach to raise the level of cognitive thinking required for the class.

Students examine matrices and Venn diagrams as graphic organizers for their solution methods. First, students are given a logic problem as a warm-up. Then the various solution methodologies are discussed and presented. Students discuss which methods they used and which appear to be most efficient. The purpose of the discussion is to have students understand the value of a matrix for analyzing problems. Then students engage in a WebQuest to learn about the use of Venn diagrams (see http://www.shodor.org/interactivate/activities/ShapeSorter/?version=1.5.0_06&browser=MSIE&vendor=Sun_Microsystems_Inc.). In the related homework they compare and contrast the two problem-solving methodologies to determine when one should be used rather than the other. Students have to solve two problems, one that is suited to the use of a Venn diagram, the other to a matrix. Students have to analyze the problems to determine which is which. Students then examine the characteristics of the problems to reflect on how their thinking caused them to figure out which solution strategy was appropriate. Students also have a Venn diagram problem that is different from the type they saw in class so that they will have to adapt the strategy to solve the problem. Too frequently in math I teach in a contextualized framework in which the algorithm to be used in problem solving is readily apparent. This lesson affords the students an opportunity to strategize and select from different problem-solving skills as necessitated by the task.

Assessments for Lesson 6 include the following:

- Individual open-ended, extended response
- Group open-ended extended response: Venn diagram exploration questions
- Individual problem-solving questions: Homework worksheet

Keeping the Habits of Mind in Mind: Continued Use of the Habits

From time to time, particularly when one of the habits is related to some aspect of the work we are engaging in, we will return to and discuss the habits using a threaded discussion on a blog (on the Internet). The purpose of the discussion is to review the habit and analyze how it is manifested in the work we are doing. For example, in algebra I emphasize error analysis as a learning tool using checks and identification of errors in work. This would be an appropriate time to enter a threaded discussion about striving for accuracy and precision. I love using a quote from Confucius as a discussion point: "A man who has committed a mistake and doesn't correct it is committing another mistake." Another example occurs when we are examining the three views of a function (graphic, algebraic, and word forms of relationships). This is an appropriate time to discuss thinking flexibly and to have students test themselves to identify learning styles.

When we begin work on our first content unit, we start with a goal-setting and achievement strategy worksheet. We focus on the seven habits that we selected. We close the unit with a self-assessing reflection on the unit. This would be an appropriate time to discuss goal setting and self-assessment.

Managing impulsivity is a great habit to focus on when engaging students in a reflective discussion of any conduct issues that require attention in the classroom. This habit provides a familiar and ready means to afford students an opportunity to regulate and modify their own behavior.

A Blueprint for Teaching

Adopting the Habits of Mind as the framework for instruction facilitates my development and implementation of "process education" in mathematics. It affords me a blueprint for teaching my process standards, developing units and lessons that are driven by cognitive tasks that demand skillful thinking, and creating essential questions for units that are premised on higher-order thinking skills and deeper understanding. Furthermore, the habits unify my efforts in process development, social/ emotional development, and management of students.

Reference

Costa, A. L., & Kallick, B. (2000). *Discovering and exploring habits of mind*. Alexandria, VA: ASCD.

17

Demonstrating Habits of Mind in the Interactive Notebook

Barbara Owens

A classroom culture is defined by signals in the environment, the practices of the teacher, and the response of the students to those practices. My high school classroom culture in Larkspur, California, clearly reflects Habits of Mind, Understanding by Design, and differentiated instruction. The cultural characteristics include simply getting started with the Habits of Mind, using the interactive notebook, engaging in the Socratic seminar, and recording the process of a writing workshop. The Habits of Mind provide a guide for how students behave intelligently when they don't know what to do. In our high school, too many of our students don't know how to "do school."

The physical layout of the classroom instantly communicates values and methodology. In my room, students sit at tables of three or four. Students typically change groups after each grading period. The formation of a cooperative group begins as the individuals share contact information. Students can then contact each other for details of an assignment that students diligently record in their planners. The foursomes, easily converted to dyads, collaborate through note sharing, discussions, jigsaws, and small-group projects or presentations. By the end of the first semester, all students have worked closely with each other. From that first exchange of contact information, students begin participating in the habit of thinking interdependently, a fundamental intelligent behavior required for students to acquire understanding as they read challenging text and discuss and write about complex ideas. These small groups also provide an opportunity for all students—particularly English language learners and special needs students—to interact in groups with diverse abilities and learning styles.

From their seats at any table, students can read posters and signs naming the Habits of Mind. These are mounted on the wall above and behind where I stand to give directions. With a wave of my hand, I can gesture to indicate which habit we are using at any given moment. Also at the front of the classroom stands an easel with a flip chart where I date and record all instruction and assignments each day. As a class we can follow the sequence of the lessons, referring back to the previous days, weeks, or even months of instruction or agreements made.

Those easel posters reveal lesson designs based on constructivist theory that I've been working with since I first used Art Costa and Bena Kallick's early work in critical thinking. The cycle of inquiry informs the process for developing students' work as well as the work I do in collaboration with several of my colleagues. The question that has compelled my own professional cycle of inquiry is this: How does the learning community create, develop, and preserve Habits of Mind that dispose students to higher levels of thought and literacy? The answer I have found that leads to the most success is using the *interactive notebook*.

The Interactive Notebook

What is the interactive notebook? Simply stated, it's a double-entry journal. This low-tech, inexpensive method is based on a standard 8½-by-11-inch spiral-bound notebook in which students write daily on both right and left pages. As a platform, both pages create a whole that records a variety of thought processes and skill development in reading, writing, speaking, and, by implication, critical thinking. One page is devoted to note taking; the other, to note making or responding to the material on the opposite page. The margins frame both pages with Habits of Mind labels that signal the presence of evidence of that habit.

For example, to engage and motivate 9th grade students to read challenging text such as Dickens's *Great Expectations*, I ask students to keep a process log of how they are developing strategies to persevere and comprehend. On the left page, we label that process "metacognition." Similarly, in Advanced Placement Language and Composition, where former 10th graders begin a first-year college-level (13th grade) English class as juniors in high school, the notebook provides what will become the review text for the entire course and the AP exam taken in May. The AP notebooks show labeling of virtually all the Habits of Mind.

The Socratic seminar requires students to use both pages for the entire process. Although a Socratic seminar can take many forms, basically it is a student-led discussion. Students, not the teacher, are responsible for the content and the pacing. Discussants have responsibility for maintaining the conversation, inquiry, exploration, and analysis of text without having to take notes. Observers, on the other hand, write careful notes on the right pages of their notebooks on what they hear.

The seminar provides opportunities to practice a number of Habits of Mind: listening with understanding and empathy, applying past knowledge, using the senses, thinking interdependently, managing impulsivity, thinking flexibly, questioning and posing problems, and striving for accuracy. On the left page, all students respond to a series of standard questions designed to elicit metacognition: What worked? Why? Who made the most memorable contribution? Why? What needs improvement? What are you going to do about it for next time? What was it like for you as an observer? A participant? Why did you choose the role of observer instead of participant? Why did you choose both roles? Why did you choose to participate?

The writing workshop format also uses both right and left pages of the interactive notebook. Typically, the brainstorming, outline, and first and subsequent drafts go on the right pages, and students use the left pages for process analysis, peer response or feedback, and planning. The workshop provides opportunities to practice such Habits of Mind as metacognition, questioning and posing problems, striving for accuracy, thinking interdependently, creating, imagining and innovating, and finding humor.

Student and Parent Feedback

Graduates from my English classes who are attending institutions such as Harvard, MIT, American University, UC Berkeley, UCLA, Princeton, Stanford, and Yale, among others, have reported that they use the interactive notebook process routinely in their coursework. One international studies major declared the interactive notebook "pure genius." A senior mathematics major at MIT returned for a visit and confessed, "I had to tell you in person that I finally 'get' the notebook." Another district graduate who teaches in a lower-performing high school in an adjacent county recently e-mailed this message: "I think the highlight of the semester was when a kid . . . who flunked the fall semester raised his hand as we were about to start a new book and asked, 'Can we do the journals again?'" The effectiveness of this process for the AP students became strikingly clear when first-time scores showed a 100 percent pass rate in an open-access class.

During the summer a parent sent an e-mail message to the superintendent and the principal to express her gratitude for her 9th grader's significantly improved literacy skills as measured by the state test results, as well as the student's improved social interaction skills.

Creating an Archive

Daily practice of the Habits of Mind helps students read challenging text, analyze it, and write about it or about other complex ideas. The written record of those efforts in the interactive notebook builds students' self-esteem, intellectual stamina, and confidence. The notebook is the archival artifact of a classroom culture that encourages the growth of intelligent behaviors in our young people.

18

Habits of Mind and a Journey into Student-Initiated Learning

Damian Baynes

Education is life, not a preparation for life.

—John Dewey

Within months after I began my first mainstream education placement, three significant factors converged, setting me on my current path of educational discovery and eventual use of the 16 Habits of Mind. First, the school where I was teaching—the Poonindie Community Learning Center in Poonindie, South Australia—provided an environment that emphasized learning and leading. The principal of the school, Morna Shane, had created this style of leadership, and it continued when Deb Hemming became the principal. Both Morna and Deb had demonstrated such qualities as *passion*—being energized by their beliefs regarding the possibilities, a fundamental ingredient to enable others to join the process; and *vision*— creating a shared vision of the possibilities. And through their *actions* they demonstrated a dedication to their beliefs by encouraging a climate of learning, risk taking, exploration, implementation, and a commitment to improved learning outcomes. Each of these qualities is needed to produce a culture of educational change and development—one in which I would feel enabled to take on a role of leading the process of change and curriculum development, both in my class and at the site (Fletcher, 2004).

The second significant factor was my reading an article by Arthur Costa and Robert Garmston (1998) titled "Maturing Outcomes." I knew that I wanted to broaden the focus of my teaching so that outcomes and activities would include learner dispositions — habits of mind and states of mind — in addition to subject-matter content (a process I am still working on). Reading this article laid the groundwork for what Arthur Costa would call "visioning" — that is, my understanding of what could be began to develop, and I began with a goal in mind.

The third significant factor influencing my teaching practice and the perception I had of myself as a professional came about after visiting a school engaged with student-initiated learning. I returned to my own site and implemented aspects of their program; but a valuable lesson ensued, for I did not own that process of change. Although it is appropriate to learn from observing others, when it comes to implementing our own actions, the last thing we need is to borrow someone else's "how-to list" or sequence of lesson plans. Instead, each of us has to take our own first steps (Lundin, Paul, & Paul, 2003). If we are to be professional about teaching and learning — and if we want to prevent emerging theory and initiatives such as Costa and Kallick's 16 Habits of Mind from being reduced to the status of fad and being discarded when the next "new thing" comes along — then we must develop our understanding of the theory underpinnings. Only then can we ensure a credible long-lasting implementation based upon the varying needs of our particular learners.

And my vision began to be reflected in my practice as I began using student-centered principles. I should mention that these reflections on my teaching practice and what I describe as occurring in my classroom did not happen all at once; and for the purposes of this chapter, I am not sequencing each development. What follows is a reflection on what occurs in my classroom currently and how I believe the Habits of Mind are being developed. It represents three years of development and is still evolving, for if we are serious about educational change and development, there is no end point. There is no wiping of the brow and congratulating oneself for having "done" the Habits of Mind. It should also be noted that my class is a 5/6/7 class, and so I have three years to develop the Habits of

Mind with my students. The significance of this fact is underscored by the following observation by Costa and Kallick (2000):

> Experience tells us it takes three to four years of well-defined instruction with qualified teachers and carefully constructed curriculum materials for the habits of mind to "succeed." After three to four years in a school, we've started to observe significant and enduring changes in students' behavior. (p. 3)

Of course, few of us have the opportunity to have the same students for three years, and so it becomes imperative that the Habits of Mind be adopted across a whole site to ensure effective development throughout the formal educative years of our children.

I also have the added bonus of the older students mentoring the younger students in the appropriate use of the habits as they engage with their learning. According to the proponents of cognitive motivation, recounting of those past experiences by the older students inspired the younger students (Cagne, Yekovich, & Yekovich, 1993).

Building a Vision Around the Habits of Mind

Just as it is important for educators and parents to develop a shared vision for a school, so, too, should students construct their own vision as to what they want to get out of their education. At times we should slow down the learning process and discuss what it is we are trying to achieve, for when we have a shared understanding, the learning moves forward in leaps and bounds (Pace Marshall, 2003).

After spending some time unpacking the Habits of Mind and relating them to the educational experiences the students encounter in the classroom and in their lives outside the school, we set about creating a class vision built around the 16 Habits of Mind. We have taken the habits and put them into our own words and in a context relevant to our classroom; we personalize our vision. As noted by Lundin, Paul, and Paul (2003), "A vision comes alive only when it is personalized by those who work in the vision" (p. 92).

Although my students may not be able to recite all of the Habits of Mind and use the language as articulated by Arthur Costa and Bena

Kallick, they are developing an idea as to where the habits fit in their vision for their schooling. An ongoing question of mine has been whether students should be able to recite the Habits of Mind in a language that tends to be quite unnatural to the child learner, or whether I should continue as I have been doing and develop teaching and learning experiences and a classroom culture that have the Habits of Mind embedded within the educative process without requiring students to memorize the list of habits. This is not to say that the class is void of dialogue around the Habits of Mind. Indeed, dialogue around the habits occurs within the context of the learning, as we seize opportunities to reinforce appropriate examples.

The Student-Initiated Learning Project

Perhaps the centerpiece of my teaching and learning, and what most obviously fosters the Habits of Mind, is a student-initiated learning program. Student-initiated learning is an outcome as well as a process. The learner gains the skill of engaging in self-directed learning. It is a process in which individuals take the initiative with or without the help of others in diagnosing their learning needs, establishing prior knowledge, formulating learning goals, identifying human and material resources, choosing and implementing appropriate learning strategies, and evaluating learning outcomes. Thus it is a process that encourages the development of the Habits of Mind:

> The habits of mind are most evident when we ask students to manage their own learning. Consider all the different habits of mind involved when we ask students to choose the group they will join, the topic they will study, and the ways that they will manage themselves to meet a deadline. Every occasion of self-directed learning is a rich opportunity for students to practice the habits of mind. (Costa & Kallick, 2000, p. 5)

Choosing a Topic

Increased student choice in terms of topics to be studied and goals that are set results in a more effort-focused learning environment (Cagne, Yekovich, & Yekovich, 1993). By allowing students to choose the topics they wish to study, we as educators are encouraging relevance for the learning. For me, motivation through relevance is not about simply working with topics that relate directly to the learners' world of familiar knowledge (such as favorite TV shows, skateboarding, or pop stars, though such topics do provide an entry point for students new to the process) or simply reproducing biographical and historical information. Rather, motivation through relevance comes about through engagement in authentic, real-life learning topics, topics related to issues or dilemmas in the real world.

I have found that as students mature as learners, the topics they choose to engage with mature also, as does the depth of engagement. (It is not unusual for a 7th grade student to produce a 5,000-word research project incorporating both primary and secondary sources of information and exploring multiple points of view.) They still may choose a topic such as surfing, but they would begin to explore such things as popular culture through surfing. However, more often than not they select topics that are generally outside the world they are familiar with—topics such as cloning, genetically modified products, deforestation, or terrorism—or they explore the relationship between science and the mysteries of the world, or the idea of beauty. They choose topics that indicate *responsible risk taking* as they venture into a world they are unfamiliar with. Of course, my role becomes that of facilitator, moderating the process, encouraging appropriate learning strategies, and encouraging use of effective learning behaviors. More often than not, such learning becomes a voyage of discovery both for the child learner and for me.

Brainstorming Prior Knowledge

Once a topic has been selected, students are required to brainstorm their prior knowledge about their chosen topic. During this phase the students are developing the habit of *applying past knowledge to new situations*. They are constructing their starting point for the learning that will follow. For example, one of my 7th grade students, Jessie, chose to tackle the topic of cloning. She really had little knowledge of the topic other than having heard about Dolly the sheep and a mule cloned in Idaho, both of which had been the topic of stories reported in the mainstream media.

Formulating Questions to Investigate

In the next part of the process, the students construct the questions they are planning to investigate; this stage thus involves *questioning and posing problems*. The questions need to be framed within the context of a past investigation, a present investigation, and a future investigation. The students are expected to develop as many questions as are practical during this phase. They also need to ensure that they investigate different points of view on their chosen topic with the questions they are posing, thus emphasizing the habit of *listening with understanding and empathy*. For example, the following are some of the questions Jessie explored:

- What are the different types of cloning?
- Why clone?
- How is animal cloning done?
- Should we clone extinct animals, and how could this be done?
- What stage are we at in the cloning of humans?
- Should we clone humans?
- What effects will cloning have on society?

She investigated the history of cloning, including the information related to Dolly the sheep and the mule cloned in Idaho; the potential health benefits to humans through cloning; and George W. Bush's comments on cloning. She reviewed two movies—*Jurassic Park* and *Gattaca*—exploring whether the premises of the stories were possible or realistic. She interviewed school staff and family members and explored her own thoughts on the topic. As one can imagine from this example, the students' investigations led to some stimulating discussions in class.

Identifying Resources

After constructing their questions, students are asked to identify where they will be gathering their information from—the resources they will be using. Because the students have not begun their research at this stage, they often are required to *think flexibly* and be open to new directions and the need to change as they actually get into the research. Students are also asked to use both primary and secondary sources of information.

Jessie found the majority of her information on the Internet and in newspaper articles. By interviewing a parent and a teacher from another class, she drew them into her education. It should be noted that the students in my class have access to all of the resources available in the school and are encouraged to use both human and material resources in the wider community. This has implications, in that all staff need to either be teaching with a similar methodology or understand the process, because there is potential for some staff to be uncomfortable with students using resources such as the photocopier as required.

Final Planning Steps

In the next step, students are required to choose the means by which they are going to present their research. This phase has the students considering what they are researching and how to communicate their work most effectively. In essence, they are using the habit of *thinking and communicating with clarity and precision*. Students like Jessie, who generate large amounts of information, frequently choose to use a computer-created book format to present their work, which results in some very professional-looking publications.

Students are then asked to identify the new learning that they will be pursuing. This, of course, requires that they build upon what they already know—their prior knowledge. I have found this part of the process to be quite difficult for students, but I feel it is well worth persisting with. This may be due to the possibility that in their past, they were not asked to draw upon past experiences and to link those experiences to their new learning.

Students then decide what they would like assessed. It is hoped that they would include any areas of their learning that they know they need to develop.

Most students experience difficulty with this multistep planning process; but as they begin to be able to plan their learning in this way, I believe they are well on the way to effectively using the Habits of Mind. As a final planning step, the planned learning episode is then negotiated with the teacher to ensure an appropriate level of challenge. The level of challenge is established just above the learners' current level of competence, scaffolding them from what they know and have heard of, into the unknown. For Jessie, this involved drawing her attention to potentially useful movies that would help her to explore the relationship between fiction and real-life scientific and technological advancements, and helping to construct such investigations as the effects cloning will have on society.

As part of this process, students may choose whom they are going to work with. Thus, as they work with other students under the guidance of the teacher, they are developing the habit of *thinking interdependently*.

Because this work represents a significant challenge for the learners, they must be *persistent* to complete the investigations by the negotiated due date. Generally students have one term (10 weeks) to plan, complete the investigations, conduct their oral presentations, and go through an assessment process. Students have approximately six hours in class each week to work on their investigations.

The Assessment Process

Once the planning phase has been completed, the students then have their peers review their plans to receive critical constructive feedback. This also allows the students to gain experience in providing constructive feedback.

The assessment process is multifaceted; it incorporates both self-assessment and assessment by the teacher. The students reflect on their learning using guiding questions based on Edward de Bono's (1985) six thinking hats, a process that enables the students to begin thinking about their thinking (metacognition). De Bono's six types of thinking are related to colored hats (white = facts, red = emotions, black = negatives, yellow = positives, green = creative, blue = process control). Both the students and I then assess their time management throughout the learning episode using a rubric as the assessment tool. By assessing the students' time management, I am hoping to reinforce the habits of *persisting* and *managing impulsivity*. In another facet of the assessment process, both the students and I use another rubric to examine whether they have followed through with their plan. I have found that students tend to wander off track with their research or want to pick up on their neighbor's topic because it seems so much more exciting than what they are working on. Therefore, in essence we are further developing the habits of persisting and managing impulsivity. The final piece of assessment relates to what the students indicated they wanted assessed during the planning stage.

Throughout the research project the students are *striving for accuracy* in both the information they find through their research and in the written communication of their findings. Of course, the writing also requires *thinking and communicating with clarity and precision.*

The Presentation of Results

The students are required to give a presentation to the rest of the class based on their chosen topic of study. They are encouraged to share written information, to use a variety of visual aids, and to involve the audience in some form of interactive activity. The students are assessed by a teacher using some basic public-speaking principles. A student member of the audience provides critical feedback in terms of what was done well, what could have been improved, and what the person providing the feedback would have done differently. Another member of the audience is required to develop a number of probing questions for the speaker. The presenter then reflects upon the whole process.

Once the students become comfortable with the process, some excellent presentations usually ensue. Again, having a group of students for up to three years is highly beneficial. I am able to gradually develop the necessary skills without rushing the students into situations they find uncomfortable. As one can imagine, almost all students are frightened of speaking formally in front of their peers for any length of time. Throughout the planning and presentation processes, a great many Habits of Mind are being used and developed.

Expanding the Use of Student-Initiated Learning

Although student-initiated learning represents a process approach to education rather than being content driven, I became aware that it had the potential to become the educational equivalent of the game Trivial Pursuit. At the same time I began considering the concept of the worlds we know as discussed by Julia Atkin (2001), with World 1 representing our innate self, World 2 consisting of our direct experiences, World 3 representing the world that we have heard of, and World 4 representing the world unknown to the learner. My fear was that students could potentially just oscillate between Worlds 1 and 2, with an occasional sojourn into World 3 with their choice of learning topics.

So it was that I introduced weekly media studies and weekly writing and discussion. As a result of these teaching and learning episodes, students examined topics of local and global significance on a weekly basis. The media studies had students examining newspaper articles using the following questions to guide their thinking and discussion: Who created the news? Where has the news happened? What are the facts and opinions reported? Why has the news been reported? What can we learn from the article? What other questions should have been asked and of whom? What are my thoughts on this topic at this point in time?

Soon I noticed the students becoming far more aware of what was happening in the world around them, as they suggested the following as potential topics for discussion writing: The Live Sheep Trade; Cloning Humans; Aid for Developing Countries; Plastic Bags; North Korea; Year 12 Exams; The Future of the Tuna Industry; Water Restrictions; Insurance—Taking the Fun Out of Playgrounds; Stem Cell Research; Forever Young—Our Obsession with Beauty; The Elderly and Driving Tests; Life on Mars—So What If There Is?; and Iraq—Was It Worth It? I also noticed that a number of students were picking similar topics of study for their research projects. Like the research projects, the discussion writing assignments provide opportunities to develop some of the Habits of Mind, including *questioning and posing problems, listening with understanding and empathy, thinking about thinking, thinking flexibly, thinking and communicating with clarity and precision*, and *striving for accuracy*. The pieces of writing are assessed using negotiated criteria in the form of a rubric.

The Habits of Mind as a Tool for Student Reflection

As the student-initiated learning program was being developed, I began exploring the topic of optimism and how optimistic behaviors can be developed, which in turn prompted my interest in students' perceptions of themselves as learners and how this affects their ability to engage in the learning process. Cagne, Yekovich, and Yekovich (1993) state:

Students' thoughts about the causes of success and failure influence their motivation . . . if students think that failures are due to
lack of effort, and if successes are due to effort, and if they see
themselves as hard working, they will persist longer in achievement situations. (p. 443)

My dilemma then became that of finding a tool through which students could reflect upon their learning selves to modify their learning
behaviors. It was at this point that my interest in the writings of Arthur
Costa shifted from the article "Maturing Outcomes" to the 16 Habits of
Mind of effective learners. Using the 16 habits, I constructed questions
and indicators that helped the learners to reflect on their learning and
their attitudes toward learning, to highlight the behaviors of effective
learners and hence the learning behaviors expected of them, and then to
begin to modify their own learning behaviors. I use the term *behavior* at
this point because I believe that students first must make a conscious decision to engage in these learning behaviors, and only through constant
revisiting and acting with these behaviors will the behaviors become a dis-
position or a *habit* and then to begin to modify their own learning behaviors. See Figure 18.1 for an example.

Through my interest in students' perception of themselves as learners, I have essentially ended up with something akin to an action research
model. The students engage with the learning, reflect on their outcomes
and their learning habits or behaviors, and then are able to observe what
they need to develop to experience further success. I am also able to use
this information to begin modifying the teaching and learning processes
in the classroom.

I must admit that I am still developing this aspect of my teaching practice, but at this stage it looks promising. For example, having taught Jessie
for three years, I was able to see her grow into a tremendously motivated
learner, exhibiting nearly all of the Habits of Mind on a daily basis. As a
teacher it is very uplifting to work with a group of learners who are aware
of their learning behaviors and who truly engage with the learning process.

There are many other aspects of classroom work and culture that are
less obvious for the development of such Habits of Mind as *finding humor,*

FIGURE 18.1

Helping Students' Awareness and Self-Assessment of Their Habits of Mind

Thinking About Thinking	Most of the Time	Sometimes	Not Yet
I can describe my previous learning and plan my new learning to build upon it.			
I can identify the areas of my learning that I need to develop.			
I can describe the new learning that I will be doing.			

When have you demonstrated this Habit of Mind? _____

_____

When have you seen this habit in other people? _____

_____

What could you do to improve this habit in your learning? _____

_____

gathering data through all senses, and *responding with wonderment and awe,* but that are of equal importance. These include me, the teacher, being lighthearted and allowing a naturally lighthearted atmosphere to pervade the learning environment while playing down many minor incidents in the classroom that might otherwise be escalated; having a strong and respected student voice; using a shared decision-making process; showing respect for each other and for ourselves; creating an emotionally safe environment conducive to risk taking, lots of group work, much dialogue, and authentic and constructive feedback; being aware of the stories we tell in the classroom as these stories become our reality; and being passionate about what we are doing.

The last element, being passionate about what we are doing, is noteworthy; for passion is contagious, and those around us will be more inclined to enter into an educational journey of continuous learning with us if they see that we truly believe in what we are doing. Pace Marshall (2003) said it well: "We ourselves have to first become that which we want others to become."

References

Atkin, J. (2001). *Teaching for effective learning*. Paper presented at a Learning to Learn conference, Adelaide, South Australia.

Cagne, E., Yekovich, C., & Yekovich, F. (1993). *The cognitive psychology of school learning*. New York: Addison Wesley Longman.

Costa, A., & Kallick, B. (2000). *Activating and engaging habits of mind*. Alexandria, VA: Association for Supervision and Curriculum Development.

Costa, A. L., & Garmston, R. J. (1998, Spring). Maturing outcomes. *Encounter: Education for Meaning and Social Justice, 11*(1).

de Bono, E. (1985). *Six thinking hats*. London: Pergamon.

Fletcher, T. (2004). *Heads up 21*. Paper presented at a conference of the South Australian Center for Curriculum Leadership, Victor Harbour, South Australia.

Lundin, S., Paul, C., & Paul, H. (2003). *Fish sticks!* London: Hodder and Stoughton.

Pace Marshall, S. (2003). *A new story for learning*. Paper presented at a Learning to Learn conference, Adelaide, South Australia.

19

Increasing Alertness:
Teaching Habits of Mind for Transfer

James Anderson

As we work with the Habits of Mind in our classrooms, we should focus on helping students become more masterful and to develop more mature Habits of Mind. Merely setting tasks that require using the Habits of Mind is not enough. Our curriculum design and our pedagogy must allow students to improve and develop their Habits of Mind.

In our work, Art Costa, Bena Kallick, and I have identified five dimensions in which the Habits of Mind can be developed. These five dimensions are fully described in *Learning and Leading with Habits of Mind* (Anderson, Costa, & Kallick, 2008). Essentially we argue that for students to develop their Habits of Mind, teachers need to be engaging them in tasks that allow them to (1) explore the meaning of the habits by having more complex understandings and being exposed to a wider range of examples and analogies, (2) expand their capacities by developing a wide repertoire of skills and strategies, (3) extend the value they place on the habits, (4) build commitment toward using and developing Habits of Mind, and (5) increase alertness to situations when it is appropriate to use (or not use) a particular Habit of Mind. In this chapter, I focus on classroom strategies that help teachers develop a student's ability to become increasingly alert to opportunities to apply the Habits of Mind.

When someone becomes masterful at the Habits of Mind, he or she is adept at applying the habits in a wide range of contexts, including familiar, novel, simple, or complex. These masterful individuals recognize, often subconsciously, certain cues in a task or situation that indicate the opportunity to engage in one or more Habits of Mind. As teachers, we are able to design our curriculum and pedagogy in such a way that makes it more likely that students become alert to these cues, and hence more able to transfer their application of the Habits of Mind to a wider range of contexts.

Robin Fogarty and colleagues have provided a model that allows teachers to focus on strategies that are most likely to facilitate transfer. Their model (Fogarty, Perkins, & Barell, 1992) describes five bridging strategies that they claim best facilitate transfer among contexts that are very different:

1. Anticipating Applications—Developing rationale; scouting for relevant use
2. Parallel Problem Solving—Moving learning from one context to another
3. Generalizing Concepts—Extrapolating generic threads
4. Using Analogies—Comparing; finding similarities
5. Metacognitive Reflection—Reflecting on the personal meaning and application

This model is useful both to help guide the design of curriculum activities as well as to help evaluate ideas for instruction. Although Fogarty and colleagues apply the model to the teaching of content knowledge and skills, here it is applied to the Habits of Mind. The following sections briefly describe the design principles of each strategy and provide some examples.

Anticipating Applications

Design Principles. Students should be considering upcoming opportunities to use a new idea, thinking about ways to modify what they are learning to make it more relevant, and speculating on possible uses and applications. The following are examples of how to apply this strategy:

• Ask students to create "When, Why, How" charts that describe situations in which the habits would be useful. Focusing on a single

Habit of Mind, invite each student in the class to answer these questions: When would they use that habit? Why would they use it? What might it look like?

• Assign a creative writing task with the following instructions: Imagine a time when you might use this Habit of Mind. Write the story from the perspective of when you use the habit and when you don't use it.

• Have students do a character analysis in which they identify situations in which fictional characters or real people need to apply or have applied Habits of Mind. For example, they might identify the Habits of Mind that Frodo uses in his quest to destroy the ring in *Lord of the Rings*.

A further opportunity for teachers to help students anticipate applications is to simply carefully choose the language they use when introducing tasks. We sometimes find that teachers are inclined to simply tell students which Habits of Mind are most appropriate to a task. Over time, we might see this level of direction change so students are given the opportunity to discuss and recognize cues in the task that alert them to the opportunity to use a particular Habit of Mind. For example, over time we might see a teacher's language change in the following ways:

1. Direct instruction: "Students, this task will require you to use the Habit of Mind of . . . . "

2. Negotiated instruction: "Students, which of the Habits of Mind might be most useful to us as we complete this task?"

3. Identifying cues: "Students, this task requires us to . . . . So, which of the Habits of Mind are going to be most important to us in this task?"

4. Explanation: "Students, explain to us which of the Habits of Mind are going to be most important to you as you complete this task."

Parallel Problem Solving

Design Principles. Students should be solving problems using the same set of skills, or problems with similar structure, in two different areas. Often one of the areas concerns the students' personal or everyday life. Students should be associating one idea with ideas already known and exploring options and possibilities for the application of an idea. The following are examples of how to apply this strategy:

• Ask students to name the Habits of Mind required to complete classroom tasks. This simple task allows students to see how the same Habits of Mind are applied in various settings and contexts and with different subjects.

• Facilitate transfer by highlighting different activities or tasks that require the same Habits of Mind. One example is through using the Habits of Mind as organizers when negotiating or setting criteria for assessment tasks. For example, ask students, "Which habits of mind would be most important to us as we complete this assignment?" Use the top three or four habits as headings to organize your assessment criteria. When this approach is repeated in different assignments or different subjects, students are able to see how the same Habit of Mind is applied in different contexts.

Generalizing Concepts

Students should be generalizing concepts and ideas, finding common threads, and looking for principles, underlying truths or "big ideas." The following is an example of how to apply this strategy:

• Ask students to go back to the When, Why, How charts they developed with the Anticipating Application strategy and summarize their findings under each heading. For example, they can be asked to generalize the types of situations in which it would be appropriate to use a particular Habit of Mind. Questions such as these can guide their work: In general, why would you choose to use this Habit of Mind? What types of errors and problems does it help you avoid? What advantages do you gain? What types of strategies are used when employing this Habit of Mind?

Using Analogies

Design Principles. Ask students to find examples or exemplars that reflect common principles or applications. The following are examples of how to apply this strategy:

• Ask students to identify characters from stories, the media, or people in their lives who apply the Habit of Mind in a mature or masterful way in different settings. Using nonexamples is also a powerful tool.

- Have students study various media (texts, newspapers, books, movies, commercials, the Internet, short stories, picture story books, or poems) that are potentially rich examples for helping students to become alert to cues in situations that indicate the opportunity to apply a Habit of Mind.

Metacognitive Reflection

Design Principles. Students should be reflecting upon, monitoring, and evaluating their own thinking, considering how to approach a task or to modify their thinking in the future. They should be thinking about their thinking. The following are examples of how to apply this strategy (see also Fogarty, 1994):

- Have students write regularly in a reflective journal.
- Use questions to lead guided reflective conversations with students.
- Have students use the four-step portfolio process to design portfolios.

In my experience, the four-step portfolio process is one of the most powerful means for developing metacognitive reflection. The four steps are the following:

1. Collection: Students collect evidence of learning or performance. A diverse collection of artifacts captured in a variety of media is most powerful.

2. Selection: Students select work to be included in the portfolio based on a set of criteria—for example, the work must demonstrate application of a Habit of Mind.

3. Reflection: Students reflect upon their performance in the light of the selection criteria.

4. Projection: The most important part of the portfolio process, the projection phase asks students to address the following statement: "To show improvement in this area, my next artifact will have to show that I can. . . ." Without this important step, the portfolio simply becomes a scrapbook—a static collection of artifacts, rather than a learning process.

By engaging in this portfolio process students are required to reflect on how and how well they applied a Habit of Mind, and provide evidence in the process. This process helps students develop several of the dimensions of development including the ability to recognize cues in tasks that indicate opportunities to apply particular Habits of Mind.

The Need for Transfer of Mature Habits of Mind

One of the core goals of education is for students to be able to transfer their mature Habits of Mind to situations outside the classroom. If schooling merely produces students who are good at school, then the point of schooling is lost. Through our teaching practice, students must develop not only a deep understanding of their content knowledge but also the mature Habits of Mind that are required to engage with that knowledge and solve problems effectively.

The strategies described in this chapter are just some examples of how effective curriculum design and pedagogy can lead to more efficacious application of the Habits of Mind. As we learn more about the Habits of Mind, and what it means to apply them masterfully, we are increasing our repertoire of teaching practices that challenges and facilitates students to develop in each of the five dimensions described here.

References

Anderson, J. (2004). In Owen, C. (Ed.), *Habits of mind—A resource kit for Australian schools*. Sydney: Australian National Schools Network.

Anderson, J., Costa, A., & Kallick, B. (2008). Habits of mind: A journey of continuous growth. In A. Costa & B. Kallick (Eds.), *Learning and leading with habits of mind: 16 characteristics for success*. Alexandria, VA: ASCD.

Fogarty, R. (1994). *How to teach for metacognitive reflection*. Palatine, IL: Skylight.

Fogarty, A., Perkins, D., & Barell, J. (1992). *How to teach for transfer*. Palatine, IL: Skylight.

Note: Hawker Brownlow Education Pty. in Melbourne also publishes Australian versions of the two books published by Skylight.

20

Sustaining a Focus on the Habits of Mind

Arthur L. Costa and Bena Kallick

Press on. Nothing in the world can take the place of persistence. Talent will not: Nothing is more common than unrewarded talent. Education alone will not: The world is full of educated failures. Persistence alone is omnipotent.

—*Calvin Coolidge*

As you have read through the stories in this book, you have already discovered the power of staying the course, as described by each teacher. Getting started is often easy. It does not take too much time to introduce the Habits of Mind. And envisioning the end is also easy. You would probably agree that if students graduate after having developed the Habits of Mind, they are likely to be successful citizens and workers. It is going through the middle that is difficult—remembering how important the habits are as students engage with curriculum, instruction, and assessments. This chapter describes how you can sustain your focus on the Habits of Mind to achieve lasting change.

Giving It Time

The Habits of Mind are not a quick fix. Our experiences in many schools have proved that it takes three to five years to successfully infuse the habits. This process requires well-defined instruction with qualified teachers and carefully constructed curriculum materials. Teachers and administrators will see significant, enduring change in students' behavior only after they make this substantial commitment.

We know that the amount of time on task affects student learning. This relationship is just as true for acquiring thinking skills such as the Habits of Mind. When thinking truly becomes an instructional goal, teachers and administrators will allocate more classroom time for activities in which students learn about, practice, and reflect on cognitive processes.

If you are reading this book as an individual teacher, encourage others to join you in the work that you have embarked upon. Perhaps your school would be willing to use *Learning and Leading with Habits of Mind* (Costa & Kallick, 2008) as a study book.

Conducting Action Research

Many schools focus on action research as a method for continuous examination and improvement. Action research is designed to collect data in the midst of practice. Action research has no control group, as does experimental research. Instead, the researcher defines a series of hypotheses and then collects data to better understand those hypotheses in light of ongoing practice.

Renee Affolter and Frank J. Jacques are two teacher-researchers from Sir Francis Drake High School in San Anselmo, California. They set up studies to determine how the Habits of Mind might affect their students' work. Affolter focused on the habit of questioning and posing problems. Her study demonstrated that students were far more successful at asking questions related to naming, defining, and describing and less successful with questions that required applying, evaluating, and hypothesizing. As a result, Affolter worked on these questioning skills for herself and her students.

Jacques's study focused on the habit of striving for accuracy. He was concerned that students cared only about performing, not about the content of the performance. He asked his students to demonstrate, record, and reflect on their capability to attend to precision, detail, and revision. He eventually concluded:

Folding a formal introduction of the concept of "accuracy" into a drawing/painting assignment appears to solicit better product. The overt presentation of the concept establishes an intellectual/behavioral framework that buttresses the art-making activity. It gets students to reflect on the kinesthetic experience and might possibly create a little distance between the artist and the art making, which can help to diminish inhibition in kids who feel [they] are "inadequate." (personal communication)

Action research provides a powerful structure for studying the Habits of Mind. The continuous search for new meaning through practice is one of the best ways to keep the Habits of Mind central to a school's work.

Discovering More Habits

The structure that we have provided in the Habits of Mind series offers a general framework for establishing the habits and building a learning community. As school staff members become more attuned to observing, recording, and analyzing the habits, they probably will do one or more of the following with our original list of Habits of Mind:

• Collapse some of the habits into a more concise list. For example, some groups find that *taking responsible risks, thinking flexibly*, and *finding humor* all fit together. Others find that *striving for accuracy* is similar to *thinking and communicating with clarity and precision*, and they put the two habits together.

• Discover that we have overlooked some habits that are significant to their school community. Adding to the habits and reexamining their meaning in specific contexts sustain the vitality of a staff's work. Each school operates in a specific, constantly changing context; the habits should be adapted to each school's learning community.

• Consider other habits to add to the list. For example, "thinking chimerically" might define the ability to imagine and fantasize. (George Lucas would be a fine example of someone who practices this habit.) "Thinking systematically" could be the inclination to find interrelationships and the ability to focus simultaneously on the whole as well as the parts. "Thinking transcendentally" might be the inclination to pose grand, abstract questions (What makes humans human? Why are we here? What is the nature of mankind?).

Our list of the Habits of Mind is a living document. The list is not meant to be complete or static. Educators should modify, elaborate on, refine, and evaluate the list. Together, we'll all make greater meaning through this process.

Building Continuity

Schools must sustain a focus on the Habits of Mind throughout a student's educational experience, from elementary through secondary school. Students need to see this continuity of expectations, or they, too, fall prey to the one-year-at-a-time syndrome. Students' learning will be more powerful if they see that schooling is a continuous pattern of learning that rests on the shoulders of the previous year. They gain little if they believe that their education is just a series of isolated episodes.

Work done with the Habits of Mind in the elementary school must be continued in secondary classes. The most challenging obstacle to this goal is time. Secondary teachers have so much to cover in so little time! Yet those teachers can use that time most efficiently by teaching for several goals simultaneously: content goals, process goals, and the Habits of Mind.

Content goals are a valuable vehicle for teaching the Habits of Mind. When teachers use a multilevel approach, students come to understand that experts—scientists, mathematicians, athletes, artists, authors, and historians—are familiar with a vast body of content as well as the dispositions of that discipline. These dispositions invariably include one or more of the Habits of Mind.

Orienting Teachers New to the Culture

New teachers make the greatest effort to adapt to a school's culture in the first three years they are there. If the school demonstrates a sharing culture, they will learn how to share. If the Habits of Mind guide the school's dialogue, new teachers will adapt those habits to their own work. In this context, we are using the word *new* to refer to both novice and experienced teachers who are new to a school whose culture embraces the Habits of Mind.

New teachers are more likely to use the Habits of Mind in their classroom if they see the habits valued and used in other settings. If new teachers hear rhetoric about the habits but don't see them in daily practice, they'll fear using the habits in their classroom. If new teachers see the habits used in a faculty meeting or a parent-teacher conference as well as in other classrooms, they are more likely to use the habits in their own work.

Cultural adaptation is powerful. As mentioned earlier, new teachers can change their value system within the first three years of teaching, using the values of the culture in which they are working (Louis, Marks, & Kruse, 1996). But new teachers cannot necessarily acquire the habits on their own. They must have guidance, see sample instruction, and observe the habits in other classrooms, in hallways, and at staff meetings and other professional gatherings.

Extending Our Reach

Staying the course in the midst of a chaotic environment is not easy. Schools need an anchor. We suggest that the Habits of Mind are such an anchor because they transcend content, programs, and disciplines.

The Habits of Mind ground a learning community in thoughtful processes. When schools anchor themselves with the Habits of Mind, they become *thoughtful* in the fullest sense of the word: sensitive, caring, and full of thought. These goals are why most educators enter the profession. They want to work in a thoughtful environment, to facilitate the thought of their students and their colleagues, and to make the world a more thoughtful place.

If you've read any of our other books on the Habits of Mind, you won't be surprised when we state that we have a larger, more global agenda for our work. That agenda is to make the world a better place through the Habits of Mind. We believe that each human being has the drive, potential, and capacity to continually practice and improve in the Habits of Mind. We further believe that people have the capacities to influence the many communities in which they interact, and, therefore, they can make the world a better place.

Many problems plague our world. Each day is filled with economic, social, environmental, scientific, and moral dilemmas, the answers to which are not immediately known. We envision a world that is a continuous learning community in which all people are searching for ways to live more harmoniously by thinking interdependently; listening to each other with understanding and empathy; remaining open to continuous learning; persisting; managing impulsivity; and dealing flexibly with the richness of cultural, religious, and human differences.

These changes will require persistence, problem finding, risk taking, and generating increasingly more creative approaches to solving world problems using the Habits of Mind instead of resorting to the violence, hatred, and war that humans too often use to resolve conflict. As examples, let us consider just a few of the Habits of Mind. When we speak of *listening with understanding and empathy*, we are really talking of transcending generations of ethnocentrism to truly see and value the abundant diversity of other cultures, races, religions, language systems, political systems, and economic views to develop a more stable world community. *Thinking about thinking (metacognition)* means developing a greater collective consciousness about the effects we have on each other and on the earth's finite resources so that we can live more respectfully and graciously and in balance with our delicate environment. We also look to *strive for accuracy* and congruence between our democratic ideals and our decisions and actions, and we strive to *think and communicate with clarity and precision*, regardless of what language others may speak. We seek to *think interdependently* by caring for and learning from others, helping each other manage the earth's resources in ways that link all humans into a global community.

Alan Kay (1990) says that "the best way to predict the future is to invent it." If we want a future that is much more thoughtful, vastly more cooperative, greatly more compassionate, and a whole lot more loving, then we have to invent it. That future is in our homes, schools, and classrooms today. The Habits of Mind are the tools we all can use to invent our desired vision of the future.

References

Costa, A., & Kallick, B. (2008). *Learning and leading with habits of mind: 16 characteristics for success.* Alexandria, VA: ASCD.

Kay, A. (1990, March). *The best way to predict the future is to invent it.* Keynote address presented at the 45th annual conference of the Association for Supervision and Curriculum Development, San Francisco, CA.

Louis, K. S., Marks, H. M., & Kruse, S. (1996). Teachers' professional community in restructuring schools. *American Educational Research Journal, 33*(4), 757–798.

Appendix:
Resources Related to
the Habits of Mind

Australia

- James Anderson, Regional Director for Habits of Mind, james.anderson@habitsof mind.org
- www.habitsofmind.org
- Blog: www.mindfulbydesign.org
- www.hom@ansn.edu.au/ habits_of_mind_hub

Hong Kong

- Anson and Ricky Chan, Regional Directors for Habits of Mind, brainbasedricky@ yahoo.com.hk

New Zealand

- Karen Boyes, Regional Director for Habits of Mind, Karen@spectrumeducation.com

- www.spectrumeducation.com
- www.learningnetwork.ac.nz

Scandinavia

- Marie Sandell, Regional Director for Habits of Mind, marie_sandell@yahoo.se

Singapore and Southeast Asia

- Henry Toi, Regional Director for Habits of Mind, henrytoi@buzanasia.com
- www.artcostacentre.com

United Kingdom and Europe

- Graham Watts, Regional Director for Habits of Mind, grahamcwatts@hotmail.com
- www.habitsofmind.co.uk

North America

- Michele Wells deBellis, Regional Director for Habits of Mind, michele.debellis.@gmail.com
- www.habits-of-mind.net
- www.instituteforhabitsof mind.net
- HOMkids.com

Books

- www.ascd.org

Discussion Site

- www.habitsofmind.org/learning_community1.htm

Australian National Schools Network. (2008). *Habits of Mind: A resource kit for schools* (2nd ed.). Sydney: Australian National Schools Network.

Carter, C., Bishop, J., & Kravits, S. (2008). *Keys to effective learning: Developing powerful Habits of Mind.* Upper Saddle River, NJ: Pearson.

Costa, A. (Ed). (2000). *Developing minds: A resource book for teaching thinking.* Alexandria, VA: ASCD.

Costa, A. (2008). *The school as a home for the mind.* Thousand Oaks, CA: Corwin Press.

Costa, A., & Kallick, B. (2000). *Habits of Mind: A developmental series* (Book I: *Discovering and exploring Habits of Mind*; Book II: *Activating and engaging Habits of Mind*; Book III: *Assessing and reporting on Habits of Mind*; Book IV: *Integrating and sustaining Habits of Mind*). Alexandria, VA: ASCD.

Costa, A., & Kallick, B. (2004). *Assessment strategies for self-directed learning.* Thousand Oaks, CA: Corwin.

Hyerle, D. (2009). *Visual tools for transforming information into knowledge.* Thousand Oaks, CA: Corwin.

Marzano, R. J. (1992). *A different kind of classroom: Teaching with Dimensions of Learning.* Alexandria, VA: ASCD.

Swartz, R., Costa, A., Beyer, B., Kallick, B., & Reagan, R. (2007). *Thinking-based learning.* Norwood, MA: Christopher Gordon.

Toi, H. (2006). *The Habits of S.U.C.C.E.S.S.: Nurturing intelligent people @ school @ home @ work.* Singapore: The Art Costa Centre for Thinking.

Toi, H. (2008). *Sixteen habits of highly intelligent students.* Singapore: The Art Costa Centre for Thinking.

Wiggins, G., & McTighe, J. (2007). *Schooling by design: Mission, action, and achievement.* Alexandria, VA: ASCD.

Index

Note: page numbers followed by *f* refer to figures.

Reciprocal Teaching, 129
reflection. *See also* thinking about
  thinking (metacognition)
    examples of student, 25–26
    importance of, 15
    reading strategies fostering, 131, 132f
    writing strategies fostering, 130–131,
      131f
reflective, defined, 130
risk taking, responsible
  in cooking, 12
  creating opportunities for, 21
  examples of, 34
  in physical fitness class, 149
  strategies for teaching, 61–62
  student reflections on, 80
  writing poetry and, 136, 138–140
rubrics, 29–33, 30f, 111f

scaffolding, 51–52
self-discipline. *See* impulsivity, managing
sensory pathways, gathering data
  through
    in cooking, 11
    in foreign language instruction,
      87–92
    metaphorical thinking and, 141
    in physical fitness class, 148
    strategies for teaching, 53–54
    student reflections on, 79
sight, teaching strategies using, 54
smell, teaching strategies using, 54
Socratic seminars, 192
sound
  teaching strategies using, 54
  thinking in, 73–74
striving for accuracy. *See* accuracy,
  striving for
Stubbings, Mary, 29
students
  doing with vs. dealing to, 20, 22
  as mentors, 25–26
  preparing for the future, 18–19, 103,
    116, 137, 193
success, creating, 136, 137, 145–146

Tahoma School District, 103–114, 111f,
  113f

taste, teaching strategies using, 54
teachable moments, 33–34
teachers
  doing with vs. dealing to students,
    20, 22
  efficacious, 28
  as learners, 21–22, 65
  as managers, 28
  orienting to HOM, 216–217
teamwork. *See* thinking
  interdependently
Think-Aloud strategy, 123, 124f
thinking
  cued by text, 116–117
  literal vs. abstract, teaching, 55–57
  macrocentric, microcentric, and
    retrocentric, 45
  metaphorical, 140–142
  skillful, 6, 152
  in sound, 73–74
  teaching for, 83–84
thinking, skillful
  decision making and, 171–179
  defined, 176
  graphic organizers for, 154–155,
    155f, 175f
  thinking strategy maps and, 154f,
    164, 165f, 172f
  writing and, 152–153
thinking about thinking
  (metacognition)
    in cooking, 10
    dialogue for, 30–31, 30f, 32f, 47
    improving the global community
      through, 218
    math instruction strategies, 185
    in physical fitness class, 148
    reading strategies fostering, 123
    self-assessment checklist, 204, 205f
    strategies for teaching, 46–48, 123,
      203–204, 211–212
    student examples of, 32f, 40f
    student reflections on, 79
    thinking time, using for, 22–25, 23f
thinking and communicating with
  clarity and precision. *See also*
  communication
    in composition, 168–170

About the
Editors and Contributors

ARTHUR L. COSTA is emeritus professor of education at California State University, Sacramento, and cofounder of the Institute for Intelligent Behavior in El Dorado Hills, California. He has served as a classroom teacher, a curriculum consultant, an assistant superintendent for instruction, and the director of educational programs for the National Aeronautics and Space Administration. He has made presentations and conducted workshops in all 50 states as well as Mexico, Central and South America, Canada, Australia, New Zealand, Africa, Europe, the Middle East, Asia, and the Islands of the South Pacific.

Costa has devoted his career to improving education through more thought-full instruction and assessment. In addition to writing numerous journal articles, he edited the book *Developing Minds: A Resource Book for Teaching Thinking* and is the author of *The Enabling Behaviors* and *The School as a Home for the Mind*. He is coauthor of *Techniques for Teaching Thinking* (with Larry Lowery) and *Cognitive Coaching: A Foundation for Renaissance Schools* (with Bob Garmston). He is also coeditor of *Assessment in the Learning Organization, Assessment Strategies for Self-Directed Learning*, and the Habits of Mind Series (with Bena Kallick); the trilogy *Process as Content* (with Rosemarie Liebmann); and *Thinking-Based Learning* (with Robert Swartz, Bena Kallick, Barry Beyer, and Rebecca

229

Reagan). His works have been translated into Dutch, Chinese, Spanish, Hebrew, and Arabic.

Active in many professional organizations, Costa served as president of the California Association for Supervision and Curriculum Development and was the president of ASCD from 1988 to 1989. Costa can be reached at 916-791-7304; e-mail: artcosta@aol.com.

 BENA KALLICK is a private consultant providing services to school districts, state departments of education, professional organizations, and public agencies throughout the United States and internationally. Kallick received her doctorate in educational evaluation from Union Graduate School. Her areas of focus include group dynamics, creative and critical thinking, and alternative assessment strategies in the classroom. Her written work includes *Literature to Think About* (a whole language curriculum published with Weston Woods Studios), *Changing Schools into Communities for Thinking, Assessment in the Learning Organization, Assessment Strategies for Self-Directed Learning,* Habits of Mind series, *Thinking-Based Learning, Using Curriculum Mapping and Assessment to Improve Student Learning,* many as collaborative efforts.

Formerly a teachers' center director, Kallick also created a children's museum based on problem solving and invention. She was the coordinator of a high school alternative designed for at-risk students. She is cofounder of Performance Pathways, a company dedicated to providing easy-to-use software that helps integrate and make sense of data from curriculum, instruction, and assessment. Kallick has taught at Yale University School of Organization and Management, University of Massachusetts Center for Creative and Critical Thinking, and Union Graduate School. She served on the board of Jobs for the Future. Kallick can be reached at 12 Crooked Mile Rd., Westport, CT 06880; phone/fax: 203-227-7261; e-mail: bkallick@aol.com.

JAMES ANDERSON is a former middle school teacher and curriculum coordinator at the Grange P-12 College in Hoppers Crossing, Victoria, Australia, where he was responsible for introducing and implementing a program for teaching thinking and Habits of Mind. He is the founding director and principal consultant of MindfulbyDesign. Anderson developed, launched, and led the first collaborative, generative network of educators dedicated to exploring the Habits of Mind. Since 2005, he has led the growth of this network throughout Australia, has supported hundreds of schools throughout Australia and abroad, and has helped extend our understanding of the Habits of Mind through major events like the International Habits of Mind Expo in 2007 (the first of its kind anywhere in the world). Anderson is a highly experienced and engaging presenter with experience at all levels of schooling from early learning through the tertiary level. He has presented to business audiences and consulted extensively with schools. Anderson is Australia's leading authority on Habits of Mind and the regional director of Art Costa and Bena Kallick's Institute for Habits of Mind. Anderson is endorsed to train and support schools and others in Habits of Mind. He offers consultancy and training services through his company Mindful by Design: www.mindful bydesign.com.

DAMIAN BAYNES is the Head of Junior School at the Australian International School Malaysia. Previously he taught in a small country town in South Australia and in a remote Aboriginal community on the Nullarbor Plains of Australia. He first encountered the Habits of Mind when he became interested in student-initiated learning. The Habits of Mind seemed a logical companion to such a program, and they became a tool that guided the learning in his classroom. He constructed learning tasks with the Habits of Mind embedded within them, and the habits became a means by which students were able to engage in assessment as learning, to reflect on themselves as learners, and to self-regulate their performance and set goals for future gains.

RACHEL BILLMEYER is an educational consultant who helps schools strengthen their reading education programs with particular emphasis on reading in the content areas and improving reading assessment practices. Her first major publication in the field of reading was *Teaching Reading in the Content Areas: If Not Me, Then Who?* published by McREL (Midcontinent Research for Education and Learning) in 1996. The positive response to this book encouraged Billmeyer to elaborate on her work by writing a trilogy focusing on reading content, strategies, and reading assessment. Those publications are *Strategic Reading in the Content Areas: Practical Applications for Creating a Thinking Environment*; *Strategies to Engage the Mind of the Learner: Building Strategic Learners*; and *Capturing All of the Reader Through the Reading Assessment System: Practical Applications for Guiding Strategic Readers*. Billmeyer may be contacted at rachelb2@cox.net.

KEVIN CLUNE teaches mathematics to 8th grade students at Pelham Middle School in New York and conducts professional development workshops that demonstrate his use of the Habits of Mind. Before becoming a teacher, he was a civil litigation attorney for 20 years.

ALAN COOPER is an educational consultant in New Zealand. He has taught at all levels of education in New Zealand and served as a principal for 20 years. During this time his school became the first in New Zealand to introduce both Dunn and Dunn's Learning Styles and Hyerle's Thinking Maps schoolwide. He is an accredited trainer in the Habits of Mind. Most recently he has acted as tutor and consultant to the Christchurch College of Education's postgraduate paper on multiple intelligences. He has written widely for educational publications and presented at conferences worldwide. He can be contacted at acooper@clear.net.nz.

GINA CELESTE COSTA has been a Spanish teacher and counselor at Dixon High School in Dixon, California, since 1983. She was a mentor teacher in 1991. With her department, Costa is working on developing a curriculum for her beginning and midlevel courses based on Total Physical Response Storytelling. She also teaches adult education Spanish classes in Woodland, California. Costa can be reached at gcostajones@dixonusd.org.

NICHOLAS D'AGLAS relishes classroom teaching and curriculum development. He has had a diverse career in education in Australia. Highlights include working in audience development for cultural organizations including Zoos Victoria, the National Gallery of Victoria, and the Swan

Hill Regional Gallery; and serving as president of the Education Subcommittee of the Museums Association of Victoria. He has worked in varied curriculum development roles, including acting senior policy officer for the Department of Education and Early Childhood Development and member of the consultative panel responsible for the development of curriculum guidelines for Victorian State Schools that are part of the new Victorian Essential Learnings curriculum. In his current role as head of arts and assistant curriculum coordinator, he leads the implementation of the Habits of Mind as a whole-school pedagogy at St. Albans Secondary College. He also represents his school as an active member of the Furlong Main Cluster—a group developing and implementing a mindful curriculum for preschool through grade 12.

LISA DAVIS-MIRAGLIA is a former professional developer in the Chappaqua Central School District in New York. She is certified by the National Board for Professional Teaching Standards and is a graduate of Bank Street College of Education. Davis-Miraglia recently graduated with a master's degree in Educational Leadership from Teachers College, Columbia University. Her role as a professional developer includes working with and supporting teachers in building their repertoire of teaching techniques, experimenting with a variety of frameworks for learning, and demonstrating how to put theory into practice. In her most recent work of exploring the potential of technology and the impact it will have on teaching and learning, she helps teachers "re-vision" their classrooms for the future. Davis-Miraglia may be reached at 27 Tyler Rd., Putnam Valley, NY 10579. E-mail: lisadavis@optonline.net or 845-528-0675.

MICHAEL GOLDFINE teaches 12th grade English in the State College Area School District in Pennsylvania. For more than 20 years he has dedicated himself to moving the English curriculum toward greater relevancy. He earned a bachelor's degree in elementary education from Penn State, a secondary education degree from Lock Haven State, and a master's degree in literature from Middlebury College's Bread Loaf School of English. When not reading, he enjoys running on trails on Mount Nittany or baking bread in his kitchen. He lives with his wife, Kathleen, and two daughters, Kelson and Jael. He can be reached at mfg12@scasd.org.

EMILIE HARD is the principal of Glacier Park Elementary School in the Tahoma School District in Maple Valley, Washington. She has been a principal at GPES, a school with more than 850 students, since 2000 and is one of the main authors of the elementary curriculum units. She coauthored an integrated curriculum for the district with thinking skills and thinking habits at the core. She supports this curriculum by providing demonstration lessons, teacher inservice training, and instructional coaching in her role as principal. Hard has more than 20 years of elementary teaching experience in Oregon, Washington, and Alaska. She has also served on the Washington State Math Advisory Committee and was a member of the state's Classroom-Based Assessment Committee. Hard can be reached at the Tahoma School District Office, 23700 SE 280th St., Maple Valley, WA 98038; phone: 425-432-7294; fax: 425-432-6792; e-mail: ehard@tahomasd.us.

GEORGETTE JENSON is a graduate of Wellington College of Education in New Zealand. She is the lead teacher at St. George's School in Wanganui, New Zealand, for the thinking skills program based on Costa and Kallick's Habits of Mind and David Hyerle's Thinking Maps®, and incorporating Dunn and Dunn's Learning Styles. In this role, she has tried ideas and developed classroom strategies much in demand by other teachers. Based on her background and practical experience, she is now a much sought-after consultant for Learning Network New Zealand and Spectrum Education. She can be contacted at g_jenson@ihug.co.nz.

CAROL T. LLOYD has been a secondary school mathematics teacher for more than 30 years. She retired from Cumberland County Schools in Fayetteville, North Carolina. She has conducted staff development in thinking skills, classroom management, and instructional strategies for the school system since 1992. Lloyd was a member of the Strategic Planning Committee for Thinking Skills in her district and helped develop and implement a training program on thinking skills for a system of 2,500 teachers. She has also presented on mathematics for regional and state conferences. Lloyd can be reached ctlloyd@aol.com.

MARJORIE MARTINEZ is a physical education teacher at Furr High School in Houston, Texas. In addition to her responsibilities with traditional high school classes, she teaches classes at the charter school called REACH and for the AVID program. She was a contributing member of the team that created REACH. She does not consider physical education to be "just a game." Rather, she treats physical education as a metaphor for a successful life.

NADINE McDERMOTT teaches vocal and general music in grades 6 through 12 for the Hewlett-Woodmere Public Schools in Long Island, New York. Previously, she taught grades 5 through 12 in the Bronxville Schools in Westchester County, New York, where she first integrated the Habits of Mind into her chorus rehearsals and general music classes. She has presented nationally and throughout New York State on music assessment. She currently serves on the New York State Music Association Assessment Task Force, and she is the state chairperson for Classroom Music. McDermott can be reached at 280 Mirth Dr., Valley Cottage, NY 10989; phone: 914-268-0466; e-mail: smsprin@j51.com.

BARBARA OWENS is an admitted Art Costa and Bena Kallick groupie for 30 years of her nearly 40 years of teaching secondary English language arts. She recently took the challenge of leaving a highly successful comprehensive high school and moving to San Andreas High School, the continuation high school in the Tamalpais Union High School District in California. Just as in the traditional setting, this school with a high-risk student population requires her daily use of the Habits of Mind as well as teaching them explicitly to students. Teaching, implementing, and promoting dispositions for self-directed learners, students, and teachers is the heart and soul of her work to promote literacy and thinking skills for all. Her years in special education, literacy coaching, Advanced Placement, literacy portfolio design and assessment, state and district test preparation, and staff development have prepared her for her work in teacher professional development. She lives in Mill Valley, California, with her husband and daughter.

REBECCA REAGAN is a retired 5th grade teacher in Lubbock, Texas, specializing in reading and writing. She received her bachelor of arts and master of science degrees in education from Texas Tech University. She has done extensive staff development work in the United States and abroad in the areas of critical and creative thinking and gifted education through the National Center for Teaching Thinking (P.O. Box 590607, Newton Center, MA 02459; phone: 617-965-4604; fax: 617-795-2606; e-mail: info@nctt.net; website: www.nctt.net). She is the coauthor of *Teaching Critical and Creative Thinking in Language Arts: A Lesson Book for Grades 5 & 6* with Robert Swartz and Mary Anne Kiser, and is the author of "Developing a Lifetime of Literacy," a chapter in *Developing Minds*, 3rd ed. Her personal e-mail address is rebreagan@aol.com.

KATHLEEN C. REILLY retired from teaching 10th and 12th grade English at Edgemont High School in Scarsdale, New York. She was a teacher-researcher and adapted the Habits of Mind as a frame for the cumulative writing portfolios. Her research into the Habits of Mind and their application in her classroom was funded by grants from the Edgemont School Foundation entitled "Metaphor, Cognition, and Critical Thinking" and "Developing Minds: Strategies to Teach for Thinking." Currently, Reilly is the director of training with the Tri-State Consortium. She can be reached at 211 Newtown Turnpike, Wilton, CT 06897; phone: 203-834-0067; fax: 203-761-9124; e-mail: KReillyCT@aol.com.

CURTIS SCHNORR is the supervisor of elementary education and the Extended Enrichment Program for Carroll County Public Schools in Westminster, Maryland. Previously he was a school principal for 22 years. He spent seven years as principal at Friendship Valley Elementary School, helping to create a "home for the mind." He has been a presenter at state and national conferences on incorporating the Habits of Mind into a school culture. Schnorr can be reached at 517 Washington Rd., Westminster, MD 21157; phone: 410-876-1807; e-mail: ctschno@k12.carr.org.

NANCY SKERRITT is the assistant superintendent for teaching and learning in the Tahoma School District in Maple Valley, Washington.

She has worked in the district for nearly 20 years and has developed the district's thinking skills curriculum. She has designed and published a training model for writing integrated curriculum with thinking skills and Habits of Mind as the core. Skerritt has conducted workshops in curriculum integration and thinking skills instruction. She is a member of the Washington State Assessment Advisory Committee, which is implementing a statewide performance-based assessment system. Before her work in curriculum development, Skerritt was a secondary language arts teacher and a counselor. Skerritt can be reached at the Tahoma School District Office, 25720 Maple Valley/Black Diamond Rd. SE, Maple Valley, WA 98038; phone: 425-432-4481; fax: 425-432-5792; e-mail: nskerrit@tahoma.wednet.edu.

Related ASCD Resources: Habits of Mind

At the time of publication, the following ASCD resources were available (ASCD stock numbers appear in parentheses). For up-to-date information about ASCD resources, go to www.ascd.org.

DVDs

How to Spiral Questions to Provoke Student Thinking (#605122 DVD)
Learning to Thinking . . . Thinking to Learn: The Pathway to Achievement (DVD and user guide #607087)

Networks

Visit the ASCD Web site (www.ascd.org). Under About ASCD, follow the links to Networks for information about professional educators who have formed groups around topics, including "Character Education," "Overseas and International Schools," "Brain-Based Compatible Learning," and "Global Education." Look in the "Network Directory" for current facilitators' addresses and phone numbers.

Online Courses

Improving Student Achievement with Dimensions of Learning (#PD05OC50)

Print Products

Building Background Knowledge for Academic Achievement: Research on What Works in Schools Robert J. Marzano (#104017)
Developing Minds: A Resource Book for Teaching Thinking Arthur L. Costa (#101063)
Educating the Whole Child (action tool) John Brown (#709036)
Getting to "Got It!" Helping Struggling Students Learn How to Learn Betty K. Garner (#107024)
Learning and Leading with Habits of Mind: 16 Essential Characteristics for Success Arthur L. Costa and Bena Kallick (#108008)
A Teacher's Guide to Multisensory Learning: Improving Literacy By Engaging the Senses Lawrence Baines (#108009)
Teaching for Meaning (theme issue) *Educational Leadership* (#105028)
Teaching Students to Think (theme issue) *Educational Leadership* (#108024)

For more information: send e-mail to member@ascd.org; call 1-800-933-2723 or 703-578-9600, press 2; send a fax to 703-575-5400; or write to Information Services, ASCD, 1703 N. Beauregard St., Alexandria, VA 22311-1714 USA.